Friends*Enemies

SHEILA LOYD CAMPBELL

i

This is dedicated to the Friends (never enemies) of my youth

Ann Martin Nelson

Sue Kingsbery Porter

And in the Memory of

Boots Walker Driskill

Patricia Beard Hawkins

Absolutely no people or events in this novel are true!

Chapter One

Thirty Years Earlier

"If beauty was wealth, our bank would be the richest in the State of Texas!"

Howard Griffin arranged four chairs in front of his massive desk and smiled at the young ladies. They gave off a combined fragrance of Ivory Soap, White Rain Shampoo, and some sort of inexpensive flowery smelling cologne. "Yes, sir, we know how to grow them pretty in Bonnetville. Have a seat, girls. Sit down!"

The girls gave shy smiles and sat. He knew each of them, of course. They had all dated his son Davis at one time or another. He offered them a soda which they declined.

"Coffee then?" he suggested.

He restrained a smile as they accepted that. There were a few moments of busy confusion as they added cream and sugar, stirred to satisfaction, and sat back down. He gave them a moment to speak and then took the initiative himself.

"Ladies, what can I do for you?"

They exchanged glances and gave pink-cheeked smiles before finally nodding toward the tallest of the four. Annette Kimball.

She was the class brain though the other three were not far behind. Howard looked at her expectantly. She cleared her throat and leaned forward in her chair.

"Mr. Griffin, we want to open an account."

He frowned, his mouth twisted in an annoyed grimace.

"But I thought each of you already have accounts. I know you do, Stacy," he said. He particularly liked this sweet-natured blond. Stacy had worked for the bank for the last two years on Saturday and all during the summer. She was a hard worker, friendly and helpful to the customers, and a joy to be around. He wished his own daughter was as pleasant.

"This isn't an individual account," Annette said. "We want this to be an ongoing account where we make deposits but not withdrawals."

Howard held back another frown. Any of his people could have handled a savings account. Why had the girls insisted on seeing him, the bank president, in person?

"We can do that, can't we?" Paula Lowe asked.

Paula was the one he liked the least, and he knew he was being unfair. Her family was poor and their account was always close to empty. But she was bright and cute in an ordinary sort of way. She was the one his son Davis had dated the longest, probably all of four months.

"You want a savings account then," he said.

"Something like that," Karen Montgomery answered. "But we want it so that no one can withdraw even one cent for thirty years.   We can deposit all we want, but absolutely no withdrawals."

Howard's eyebrows arched. "A trust?"

They looked at each other, and Annette leaned closer to his desk.

"Yes, I think so," she said. "We want to open an account in all our names. We'll each deposit $25 today. Then we'll add to it each month starting in June after we graduate and gets summer jobs. That's in six weeks," she pointed out like he didn't know. "We'll add to it each month for the next thirty years. After that, we'll get together and discuss our lives. The one who has made the greatest contribution to society gets the whole pot.   With interest, we're hoping it will be $50,000."

He doubted it, but he would do the figures for them.

They completed the paper work, and each girl signed her name taking great care to make it look mature and professional. He gave them each a stack of deposit slips but no withdrawal blanks. They left his office with repeated thanks and a skip in their steps.

Over the years the money had come in. Not every girl had added $25 every month. Sometimes one would skip a month or even two or three. Then there would be a payment. Sometimes that payment was more than the $25. Howard made sure the interest was paid quarterly and that each girl received a statement so they could see their savings grow. At no time during the following years did any of the ladies come to the bank and check on the funds. Nor was he aware of either of them calling. They simply set up the account, contributed to it somewhat regularly, and otherwise forgot about it. Howard hoped to see which girl would be deemed worthy to receive the whole pot at the end of the thirty years. He hoped it would be Stacy, but he had heard that the Montgomery girl had accomplished some good things due to her financial expertise. At any rate, the funds were an asset to his bank and he was pleased to watch it grow.

It wouldn't be fifty thousand, but it would be a tidy sum even considering inflation. He wouldn't mind having that much play money. He wondered what the winner would do with her prize. Howard would have gone to some exotic island for a month and then played golf every Saturday until the last penny was gone. And he would have enjoyed every second of it.

Chapter Two

Present Day

It was time.

Davis Griffin leaned back in his chair, hands behind his head, grinning like the great quarterback he had been so many years before. He could hardly wait to see the girls again. He could think of them in no other way than girls though he knew they had aged as he had.

The Fearless Foursome, that's what they once called themselves. He probably was one of the few people who knew what a misnomer that was. They were each insecure and fearful in their own way, and he had understood them and known some of their darkest secrets. In a way, he had encouraged their fears and enjoyed doing it. Annette alone hadn't been intimidated by his charm, wealth, and sports accomplishments. They had dated only twice, and that had been enough for both of them. Davis's sister Vernye said it was because they were both control freaks with no humility and would never choose to complete with someone on their own level.

Maybe then, he thought with a grimace, but not now.

He pulled Annette's letter out again and spread the thick, expensive paper on his desk. Plain bond would never do for the woman who expected to be the next First Lady of the State of Texas.

Dear Davis Griffin,

I am sure you remember me though it has been years since we last met. I hope your father explained the trust fund set up thirty years ago by me, Paula Lowe Clifton, Stacy Winters Durfey, and Karen Montgomery Brewster.

We will be in Bonnetville October 9 through October 17. We would like to meet with you on October 10 to discuss the fund. The figure now stands at $43,629.14. We will let you know on October 17 whose name will go on the check.

We are looking forward to visiting with you.

Sincerely,

Annette Kimball Thackeray

Sure, Annie, he thought. I'll be at your beck and call.

He poured himself a cup of coffee from the coffeemaker he kept on a neat table in the corner of his office. The aroma penetrated his senses, caressing and fragrant. Nobody made coffee the way he liked it, so he made his own. Sipping the steaming brew, he stared out the window and watched the lazy traffic below. Bonnetville was bigger than when he and the four ladies had grown up and graduated from the high school on the hill. But it was far from a metropolis. There had been around 1500 people in the old days. Now because of a glass factory, a feedlot, and a few food franchises, the population had risen to about 5500. The growth had been good for his bank since it was the only one in town. But some people resented the intrusion of outsiders and the problems caused by more people. The town had voted down a bond to add on to the school, and for years no one had been in favor of raising taxes to hire more policemen and firemen and to hire an ambulance service. But finally, the newcomers had outnumbered the old home folks, and there were three new buildings added to the school. The police department boasted seventeen policemen including dispatchers. The fire department had six full time employees and there were forty volunteers, including himself, who could be assembled and ready to roll in less than twenty minutes. A small twenty bed hospital with an attached clinic had been built. There was a doctor, a physician's assistant, and eight nurses and aides who worked anywhere from twenty hours a week to full-time.

Davis gulped the rest of the coffee and stared at the mug as though wondering how it had gotten in his hand and emptied so quickly. It was the mug his daughter Jennie had given him for Father's Day when she was three. She was twenty-five now and trying to be a model in New York. Davis worried about her every day, sure she was caught up in the world of drugs and other filth. Peggy, on the other hand, envied their daughter and felt that life had cheated her.   Peggy tried to capture some of that lost life through Jennie's achievements.   Davis shook his head and turned the mug upside down on the paper napkin kept on the table for that purpose.

He returned to his chair and looked at the letter again.   He hadn't been privy to the meeting thirty years before.   But his father had told the story so many times, he felt like he knew every detail. His father had thought the pact, as the girls called it, was silly and funny and totally high school.   But he had helped them and honored his part over the years.   One of the last things Howard had said to his son before he died eight years before was, "Davis, take care of the girls' money.   Have it ready for them when they want it."

It sounded like they wanted it.

Chapter 3

Reunion

Four hearts beat a little faster, a Christmas-like excitement of anticipated surprise and the joy of unexpected adventure. Four hearts now so many years older, still throbbed and broke and mended as they had when they were teenagers.

Four souls who dreaded exposing themselves after so long, who worried that they wouldn't measure up, who feared that their failures and secrets would destroy them when nothing else had.

Four breaths sighed deeply as they neared the first hurtle – greeting the past from which they had all fled. Four smiles fixed firmly and with determination, no matter what the consequence.

They were as ready as they would ever be. Even another thirty years wouldn't soften the fates that waited. For better or for worse, it was time to honor the pact they had made so many lifetimes ago. They each hoped that the love and friendship that had bonded them would give each of them the forgiveness their betrayals would demand.

Four women who strived to achieve and prayed to overcome for they each knew their secrets had festered and would need the cleansing lance of confession to make them worthy.

It was time.

They wouldn't all be staying at the new Leisure Inn on the edge of town. Annette would because her parents were in Europe celebrating fifty-three years of marriage. Their house was being renovated, under the direction of Annette's older brother Les. He and his wife Jen hadn't invited her to stay with them, and she wouldn't have anyway. The Leisure Inn, with room service and a pool, suited her just fine.

Karen would stay there, too. The farm she had grown up on had been sold years before. Her mother had been dead for ten years, and her father was in a nursing home oblivious to anyone. Her six older brothers were scattered across the globe like dandelion seeds in the wind. Like her, none of them had settled in their home town.

Stacy would stay with a niece who now lived with her family in the house Stacy had grown up in. Stacy's mother had died over twenty years ago, and her older sisters lived in El Paso and Dalhart. Neither of them wanted to return to Bonnetville for the school homecoming. Stacy wouldn't have either if it hadn't been that magic thirty year mark.

Probably Paula would stay with her brother William and his family in their old home. Paula's parents were both gone now, too. But her brother William lived in the house and ran the propane business in town.

They had decided to meet at the hotel Friday afternoon, a full week before Homecoming Weekend. Neither woman cared a flip about returning to the scene of so many of their crimes, but they would attend the football game and later the dance. The week would be strange because all four women would be alone. Those who had a spouse had tactfully left them home so the others would not feel out of place. Their children were for the most part grown and on their own. It would be just the four of them spending the next week getting reacquainted and catching up and trying to recapture some of their youth. Then families would join them the next weekend for the homecoming festivities.

Of course, getting reacquainted wasn't the sole purpose – or even the main one – for their get-together. They would be baring their souls to determine which one got the forty thousand plus dollars they had been saving for over thirty years.

The first to arrive was Stacy Durfey. She parked her gray Lexus in the parking lot and stood looking around, wondering what everyone else would be driving and what they would be wearing. She herself had chosen a peach shade pantsuit which hid her pudginess and emphasized her coloring. Daniel loved the outfit on her, and she had learned to trust his taste.

She looked around and cringed as a brand new candy apple red Trans Am screeched into place two places down. Stacy shook her head, a tolerant smile gracing her face. There was no mistaking the tall lady who emerged from the car, stretched and yawned. The once blond now wore her hair red, very short and spiky. But the face was the same right down to the little freckles dotting her nose. Nobody else in the universe would think of wearing hot pink jeans with an oversize turquoise shirt and layers of colorful beads. Nobody else would have been able to carry off such a look, but somehow it worked for Karen Brewster.

They looked across the cars at each other and grinned.

"That you, Stacy-Pacy?"

Stacy laughed. "Hi, Karen."

They rushed to greet each other and exchange hugs.

"Have you seen Annette or Paula?" Karen asked, tapping a cigarette out of a monogrammed box and sticking it in her mouth.

"Just got here myself. I guess we can ask at the desk if either of them have arrived."

Karen blew smoke upward. She shoved her sunglasses on top of her head and squinted. "Let's see," she said. "I'm betting that fancy SUV yonder would belong to Mrs. Thackeray. And Paula would drive...hum...I don't see any Subaru wagons or Toyota pickups."

Stacy gave into a nudge of irritation with a frown. "Don't be tacky, Karen. Besides, I'm not sure Paula's staying here. She may have flown into Austin and had her brother pick her up. She may not have her own transportation. Or maybe she rented a car."

Karen shrugged, but there was a mischievous sparkle in her green eyes.

"She's the one who always preached foreign trade. Remember that argument she and Mr. Herndon got into during that one economics class. He said to always buy American, and she said we should share our wealth with other nations. I thought that was so funny because her family never had any wealth."

A ten year old small model silver Chevy pulled past, stopped abruptly, and backed up. The woman who smiled at them hardly looked any older than she had thirty years before. There was a bit of gray in her brown hair but the wrinkles around her eyes and mouth were faint. Those eyes did reflect a touch of…something. Both Stacy and Karen noticed but didn't try to pinpoint it. Nor did they mention it. Karen let out a squeal and Stacy cried, "Paula!"

The three entered the hotel, arms linked and their laughter carrying across the lobby. Seeing them, another woman rose from a chair and turned to face them. The three reached the reservation counter when they heard a soft voice behind them.

"Looking for me?"

They whirled, or tried to anyway. Bumping and twisting into each other, the trio yelled, "Annette!" and flung themselves against her.

The reunion had begun.

Chapter 4

Renewing Acquaintances

"This definitely calls for a drink!" Karen said when the hugs were complete.

"I'll drink to that," Annette said with a grin. "In fact, I have an excellent bottle of whiskey and one of rum. I'll get them and those lovely plastic glasses from my room, and we can meet at the pool."

"Just let me check in," Karen said heading back for the reservation desk. "I'll bring down a bucket of ice."

Paula and Stacy watched the other two rush off and then turned to face each other.

"Lordy, thirty years!"Stacy laughed. "Can you believe it?"

They linked arms and headed for the pool area.

"It doesn't seem possible," Paula agreed. "I know a lot has happened in that time, but it just doesn't seem that long ago. I remember everything about school, just like it was yesterday."

"Even the little explosion you and Karen caused in chemistry class?" Stacy teased.

"Ouch," Paula cringed. "All right, there may be a few things I have tried not to remember!"

They stopped before the vending machines located by the doors that led to the pool area.

"I'm not much of a drinker," Stacy said reaching in her purse. "I'll get some soft drinks and water for mixers."

"I'm hardly a drinker at all," Paula confessed. "Never liked it, never needed it. And I can get drunk on the fumes. How about I get some of these pretzels and nuts? Oohh! And chocolate bars! Does that go with booze?"

"What doesn't go with chocolate? Daniel put a sign on the wall in the den next to my exercise bike. It says, 'Every time I hear the dirty word "exercise", I wash my mouth out with chocolate.' Is that great or what?"

Paula gave a quick squeal of laugher. It was the first real laugh Stacy had heard from her.

"That's great," Paula said. "I'll have to remember that one. It's like my life's motto."

Their party drew stares from other guests, but they were interested only in themselves. They were unaware of how well they each had weathered the battles, how good they looked. They were a stunning display of middle-aged beauty, intelligence, and experience. But they were in their own little world as they rejoiced in seeing each other and didn't notice the interested glances of others.

Annette filled her plastic cup with ice, poured whiskey to almost the top, and splashed in a little bottled water. Karen used only two ice cubes and poured a full cup of whiskey. Stacy poured a Coke over ice and added a tiny bit of rum. Paula filled her cup with ice and Seven-Up.

"No booze, Paula?" Karen's question was casual but there was a bite to it.

For a moment, it looked like Paula was going to snap out a defensive reply. How many times had that happened when they were growing up? But thirty years had taught her some things.

"Don't like it," she said. "Don't need it. Don't want it. Chocolate, on the other hand," she said as she picked up a bar, "is a necessity of life. Have some."

"One of the major food groups, isn't it?" Annette reached for a piece. She tipped her cup slightly in Paula's direction and gave her a subtle salute.

Paula smiled, knowing she was being congratulated for handling Karen, something she hadn't always been able to do when they were growing up.

Their visit continued to the dinner hour when they moved inside to the restaurant and ordered the Friday night catfish special.

"I haven't had fried catfish in I can't remember when," Paula said, taking a bite.

"Me, either," Karen said. "And fried okra! Do we Texans know how to eat or what?"

The years seemed to fade away as they reminisced about old times. Though it was the first time in thirty years they had all been together, they felt as comfortable with each other as though they had never been separated.

Karen picked up her iced tea and hoisted it in the air. "A toast before we call it an evening. There's no friends like old friends. Here's to old friends!"

"Hear! Hear!" Annette lifted her glass.

The four of them clinked their glasses and sipped slowly. They sat in comfortable silence contemplating their lives, past and present. They had been through much growing up together and knew each other so well. There was a trust they never could have with others. As they watched the lights reflect off the water in the pool and listened to the country music playing in the background, they forgot the past and escaped back into a world they had sought to leave so many years before.

Chapter 5

Paula

Stacy, Karen, and Annette exchanged glances. Paula sat, chin nestled over folded hands with elbows propped on the table, and stared out the window toward the pool. Her eyes shimmered with tears, but she was lost in a world of her own.

"Paula?" Annette whispered. "Are you all right? Paula?"

Paula blushed. "I…oh, I'm so sorry! What lousy company I am! I guess I'm just tired. My mind was a million miles away."

"Want to talk about it?" Stacy asked.

Paula feigned confusion. "What? There's nothing wrong! Really. It's a long drive from Amarillo. I left at four this morning."

"Maybe we should call it a day and get together tomorrow," Annette suggested. "What about breakfast? My brother tells me there is a new restaurant out on Highway 4 that serves very good food."

"Good idea!" Paula stood so quickly her chair fell over. "Whoops. What time shall we meet?"

"Eight." Karen stood and picked up Paula's chair. "Not too

early, but early enough that we can be finished and meet Davis at the bank before it closes at noon. Is that okay with everybody?"

There was another round of hugs and Annette and Karen walked Paula and Stacy to their cars.

"Davis is expecting us at ten," Annette said. "But I can ask him to make it later."

"Do that." Karen yawned widely and loudly. "It won't take us any time. We're just reporting in, so to speak. Ten minutes before noon would give us plenty of time, and he would still be done early enough to hit the golf course."

Annette and Karen watched the taillights of Stacy's and Paula's cars as they disappeared down the road.

"Can you believe how great they look?" Annette said.

"We look pretty good, too," Karen pointed out with another yawn. "Something's bothering Paula. I don't care what she said."

"I know. But, Karen, we have to be careful how we handle her. Paula's always been the private one, the one who never spilled her guts. We may be able to help her. But if we're not careful, we'll push her away. My guess is that she hasn't gotten over the divorce from Gary."

Karen pooh-poohed that idea. "That's been almost two years ago! And she's better off without that lying, cheating--"

"He cheated?"

"Hell, yeah? Didn't you know? Some bimbo almost as young as their daughter. Paula was devastated. Felt really betrayed. Especially since they had been married over a quarter of a century.

You would think if you made it that long, it was a done deal."

Annette studied the darkness thoughtfully. "I didn't know. How do you?"

Karen shrugged. "We keep in touch once in awhile."

"Really?" Annette didn't bother to hide her surprise. "You mean more than the yearly Christmas card and an occasional birthday greeting?"

Karen nodded. "Sometimes. We've talked on the phone, dropped a few lines. We've done some emailing and Facebook. Hasn't she contacted you? She's the one who was always so good about keeping in touch, at least right after we first graduated."

Annette considered Karen's question. "I guess she did write for awhile. And always sent a Christmas card with a newsy letter and pictures. I'm sure she has never missed my birthday though I probably haven't sent her a card more than three or four times in all these years. I don't do Facebook. We don't have enough privacy as it is though Brent does have a political site. But I still should have made an effort to keep up better. I just never seemed to find time to…well, I was always caught up in so many things."

Karen led them back toward the hotel. "Yeah, I know. We're always too busy. It's a good excuse anyway."

Annette sighed. "Well, it's an excuse."

Paula pulled in the drive by her brother's house – the home she had grown up in – and locked the car. There were still lights on in the house, but she walked around to the back to the little guest cottage. William had remodeled their dad's old workshop into a small but cozy apartment complete with full bath and a small refrigerator and microwave. She was grateful that he and his wife Claire were allowing her to stay there for the week. William told her that they had fixed the guest house for her and their younger sister Jana Sue when they wanted to visit. It would also come in handy for their own children who were growing up and moving off.

Paula put her purse and jacket on the bed. She switched on the lamp over the bed but did not turn on the overhead light. The night was clear with billions of starts twinkling through the universe. It wasn't that cold for October, and there was no breeze to disturb the tranquility of the evening. She went back outside and sat on the swing that had been there since she was a child.

Her thoughts were so muddled, and she was so tired. But she was more tired inside than out and didn't know if she would ever feel the peaceful rested feeling of contentment she thought she had had until the day she found Gary with "the other woman."

She could let the tears drip down and off her face now. There would be no one to ask questions she wasn't ready to answer or express concern she could not deal with receiving. Why did everything in life have to be so hard? It seemed like she had had to fight for everything she had ever wanted. And the struggle was so hard that it didn't seem worth it when the battle was over.

Paula was the oldest child. Her dad Harold had spent his adult life going from one local job to another. He always worked, but there was never enough money to give his family all they wanted. Her mother Iona was a stay-at-home mom which was the norm rather than the exception in those days. Iona tried to bring in extra money by selling cosmetics door-to-door and babysitting. One Christmas she had baked her famous rolled spice cake, secured it in pretty plastic wrap, attached a bow, and sold them for $5 each – an exorbitant amount then. That had helped buy Christmas for her three children as Harold's salary scarcely covered the house payment, utilities and a ham for Christmas dinner.

Paula and her family attended Bonnetville Methodist Church. Religion in their home was a Sunday thing as it was for most of the people in the area. They attended church but little was done the rest of the week. There might be prayers over the meal for special events like Christmas and Thanksgiving, and the Bible was always prominently displayed on a small table in the living room. Prayers intensified when there were serious needs like lack of finances or sickness. And once to know if they should move to Waco where Harold could work for his brother-in-law landscaping. Paula had been so relieved when apparently God didn't want them to move any more than she did because the subject was dropped when her parents figured out they couldn't live any cheaper in Waco than they could in Bonnetville.

Paula could never remember a time when she didn't feel like she was more than one person. Her petite body was crowded with so many emotions and she couldn't separate them. Sometimes she was she was the nicest and most caring of her friends and sometimes she was the most hateful and bitchy. There were times she was so selfish and stingy, she wouldn't even share a candy bar with her little sister. And other days, Paula wished for richest to give to everyone who had nothing. She might be supportive and encouraging, but she could also be nasty and tear down another's achievements and dreams without even a flicker of remorse. It got to where Paula hated to look in the mirror fearing which part of her would show up. There was such a contrast of emotions bubbling inside that she never knew which one would surface. She lost count of the times her mother had told her she was the hardest child in the world to live with. Paula had never felt Iona was that easy either.

Paula twisted in the swing and dragged her foot on the ground. Motherhood had brought out the best in her, but it didn't sustain her now that the children were grown. The demons kept resurfacing when she felt particularly lonely and vulnerable. The anger would flare or the frustrations would take over, and she felt like anything she had achieved toward being the person she wanted to be would jettison right back to square one.

She sighed and twisted the swing in the other direction. For a moment she felt fifteen again and expected to hear her mother call her in for the night. Iona had died suddenly of a heart attack fourteen years earlier, and Harold died less than two years later after a short battle with cancer. She missed her mother though there had never been another person in her life that could cause her so much grief and turmoil. Iona had a knack for bringing out the worst in her oldest daughter. Paula felt that she could never measure up to whatever it was that Iona expected of her. All Paula had ever wanted was a mother who understood her fears and insecurities and accepted her for who she was. It had taken years to understand that Iona had wanted the best for her though they seldom agreed on what that was. Paula was glad that Iona never knew what a sleaze ball Gary had turned out to be. She never wanted to see that disappointment in her mother's eyes, never wanted to feel that failure in wake of her mother's ever vigilant observance.

Paula missed her dad less since they had never been that close while she was growing up. He was always busy working and William and Jana Sue were much easier to be around. She knew her dad had loved her, and she had loved him, too. But he did represent the male force that she had come to resent and despise. Until recently.

And that was the secret she didn't want to share.

Chapter 6

Annette

Annette bid Karen goodnight when the elevator stopped at the second floor and rode it on up to the fifth where her room was located. But before she reached her room, she remembered leaving her briefcase in the SUV and decided to go down for it. There were a number of things she needed to do this week regardless of it being a holiday for her. The future First Lady of Texas already had responsibilities and many demands on her time.

She tried not to be too optimistic, but Annette felt with all her heart and soul that Brent would be elected governor next fall. He planned to announce his candidacy over Thanksgiving holiday. He really wanted the office, and she really wanted him to have it. And if she was honest with herself, she very much liked the idea of being married to the governor. She wouldn't push her way into office and try to take over, but she had no doubt she would have considerable influence over her husband. They were a team.

Annette reached the elevator the same time as a young family. The mother and father looked to be in their late twenties or early thirties. Beyond a cordial greeting, Annette paid little attention to them. It was the baby the woman held in her arms that drew her attention. While the parents were Caucasian, the boy was obviously mixed race. His skin was a lovely sienna, and his eyes an alert puppy brown. His dark hair was curly but not quite kinky. His smile was enough to melt even the most frigid heart. He reached out to touch the butterfly pin on Annette's jacket.

"Oh, no, Robbie," his mother said as she pulled his tiny hand back.

Annette reached out to the child offering a finger which he took and pulled to his mouth.

"He's adorable." Annette's words were hardly audible. "How old is he?"

"Eight months." The mother's pride was evident in her smile and the kiss she planted on his cheek.

"I envy you." You have no idea how much I envy you, Annette thought. "I wish my children were still this little." She didn't really. She enjoyed the freedom that having almost grown children gave her.

"Thank you. We feel very blessed. We were able to adopt him when he was only three weeks old, and he's been such a joy ever since."

Adopted. Always a lovely option, Annette thought. Never abortion. Never, never, never kill a baby. She knew the bumper sticker said "Never, never, never shake a baby", but the sentiments were the same.

"Excuse me." The father spoke for the first time. "Aren't

you…you are Brent Thackeray's wife, aren't you?"

The politician surfaced. She offered her hand to the young man. "I am Annette Thackeray. And your name?"

"Doug Montana. My wife Marie. You've met our son Robbie."

Annette acknowledged them with a smile. "It's a pleasure to meet you."

"We hear rumors that your husband will run for governor. Is that true?"

Annette laughed. "No announcement has been made. Do you think he should?"

"Oh, yes!" This was from Marie. "We do feel he's the man for the job."

"Thank you," Annette said. The elevator stopped on the third floor. "I'll be sure to pass that along to my husband. Good night." With a final soft stroke down the baby's cheek, Annette watched the young family leave the elevator.

Once she got to her floor, Annette unlocked the door to her room and entered. She tossed the briefcase on the bed and sank into a chair. Without bothering to find a cup, she grabbed the whiskey and sipped from the bottle. Whatever made her think she could waltz back to her past and function as though her whole life was one big fairy tale with no chance of anything but a happy ending?

The years had been good for her, but she was a fighter. A survivor. Life could have turned out so differently.

She let the liquor numb the memories and mask the pain. After all these years. After over thirty years, the guilt continued to haunt and torture her. A sob escaped before she knew it was brewing, and she made her way to the phone by the bed. Only Brent could ease those doubts, chase away the demons. Only he could understand.

It was her dirty little secret, and she hoped no one ever learned of it.

Chapter 7

Stacy

Stacy was hoping everyone would be in bed when she got to her niece's house, but Nina had stayed up. Stacy greeted her with a hug, hoping her disappointment didn't show.

They sat on the couch that would fold out to be Stacy's bed and talked for half an hour before Nina finally excused herself.

As soon as the door to the den closed, Stacy dug out her cell phone and called Daniel. His voice made her lonely and homesick. Tonight he sounded tired, and immediately she worried that he was getting sick.

"Nonsense," he said when she expressed her concern. "I worked all day on my manuscript, so I am tired. But it's a good tired. I feel I have a good piece of work going here."

"I'm sure you do." She smiled, picturing him dressed in his blue striped pajamas, glasses perched on top of his head, the phone in one hand and a book in the other. "Did you eat today?"

"I...believe I did. Yes, a sandwich and some of the soup you left."

Daniel often forgot to eat if she wasn't there to prompt him.

She sighed. "Darling, you need to eat. Do I need to come home?"

"Certainly not! Stacy, you have been planning this reunion for thirty years. I want you to enjoy every moment of it."

She kicked her shoes off and curled her feet up under her.

"It's hard to enjoy most things without you," she told him. "It has been lovely to see Paula and Karen and Annette. It really has. But I miss you."

He laughed. "Precious, you've only been gone since this morning."

"I know." Her voice became the whining little girl's that always cropped up when she was feeling particularly vulnerable and especially lonely. "You are still planning to come next Saturday, aren't you?"

"Of course. I'm looking forward to it. I should have finished the first editing of the book, so I'll be ready and deserving a nice break."

"Good. I guess I should let you get back to your book. I just…I just wanted to hear your voice."

There was such a pause that Stacy wondered if he had already started reading.

"Stacy, is everything all right?"

"Of course." She could never lie to him. So she took a deep breath and spoke her words in a rush. "We're going to the bank tomorrow. Just to see Davis and prepare him for our withdrawal."

Again, there was hesitation as her husband read between the

lines. There was no fooling him.

"Stacy, you don't need to worry. It's all right. It will be fine."

She cringed as tears burned their way down her face. "I know. I guess. I just…oh, Daniel! I don't think I'll ever be able to shake this feeling until I…I--"

He sighed. "We've discussed this, darling. I'm with you whatever you decide. But I think you're being way too hard on yourself. Why don't you get a good night's sleep and see if things don't look better in the morning."

She wiped away the tears and focused on speaking with a steady voice.

"You're right as usual. Do you mind if I call you in the morning? I don't want to disturb you once you start working."

"Stacy." His voice took on a husky, endearing gruffness that stirred her every emotion. "You never need permission to call me. You never disturb me. You are the very best part of me."

"I love you so much!" She couldn't restrain the outburst. Even after all the years of marriage, he could excite and reassure her as no one else would ever be able to. "Rest well, darling. I'll call. Good night."

Despite his reassuring words, she undressed and donned a warm nightgown with anxiety still gnawing at her. It would be very hard to go to the bank tomorrow – a place she had worked while still in high school. She was afraid she would blurt out her greatest secret without thinking, and she would continue to pay for her sins even more than she had already. Then everyone would know.

Chapter 8

Karen

Karen couldn't settle down to bed. After being so sleepy earlier, she was now so keyed up that the thought of sleep was annoying. Instead, she grabbed her jacket and purse and headed down to the parking lot. Without a plan, she got in her car and drove. Bonnetville had changed so much since she had lived here. And yet, it was the same. She had mixed feelings about returning and meeting up with the friends she had shared so much with. But seeing "the girls" had been good. It had been fun, and she looked forward to spending more time with them. She hoped to spend individual time with each. She thought perhaps she would suggest that they each meet one-on-one as well as in a group.

Karen drove past Serenity Retirement Home and then backed up to pull in front of the building. She knew it was too late to go in, but she really did need to visit her father. He had been here for the last eight years, and she had seen him only once right after they "committed" him. Committed had been his word when he was still lucid enough to understand what was happening.

Poor Dad, Karen thought as she sat with the motor running.

She studied the structure. One half of the complex was indeed a retirement center where individuals and some couples lived in comfort and were attended by the staff as needed. The other side was a nursing home where people like Claude Montgomery vegetated waiting for death to claim them. How angry he had been when she had sided with her brothers and used a court order to force him into this place! At first, he had been allowed a one room apartment on the retirement side. But it had quickly become apparent that he was no longer capable of caring for himself when he forgot to remove a pan of stew from the stove and it caught fire. For his own safety as well as the rest of the residents, the staff had moved him to the nursing home.

Karen didn't know how often her brothers visited or even checked up on their father. Claude had been a proud and hardworking farmer. He had been stern and insisted on the highest integrity from each of his seven children. There had not always been good feelings between them. Indeed, he and Karen had had a falling out shortly after her mother's death of a brain aneurysm two years prior to his "commitment". Claude Montgomery thought his daughter had become a wanton woman. Too many husbands, untrained children, lack of morals she hadn't learned in his home. Growing up, she had been his little princess, his "Dolly."

Not realizing it, she sighed deeply and pulled out of the parking lot. She would have to see him, of course. But if what her brother Ronnie had told her was true, he wouldn't even know she was there much less who she was.

She drove past the country line. Bonnetville County was dry, a fact that had never bothered nor concerned her. Like all the other people in the county, she could easily drive into Cullen County for alcohol. But she wasn't seeking booze. She was looking for people. She didn't want to be alone, and she certainly didn't want to impose on her friends. All three of them seemed comfortable with themselves. She never had been despite the impression she presented.

She parked in front of Larry's Lounge and locked the car. It was probably a "membership only" club, but she could talk her way into anything. To her surprise though there was no one at the door to bar her entrance. She entered, looked around, and selected a table in the corner. It would allow her to study the place before mingling – if she chose to do so.

A waitress took her order for white wine, and Karen settled back to enjoy the music and take some time to reflect on the day. What a hoot it had been seeing the girls!

She took a cigarette and stuck it in her mouth. To her annoyance, a match immediately flared before her face. Frowning, she drew on the cigarette and blew smoke.

"Thanks." She hoped whoever thought he was coming to her rescue took the hint and left. She was surprised at the words she heard next.

"Karen? Is that you?"

She looked up and her eyes widened. "It's…it's Ryan, isn't it? Ryan Wardlow?"

"Guilty. Are you here alone?"

"For the moment."

He nodded. He had put on weight and lost a little of his thick black hair that was now streaked with gray. There were some wrinkles and his shoulders slouched a bit. But it was certainly Ryan. He had been ahead of her in school.

"Mind if I join you until your party arrives? I couldn't believe it when I saw you walk in."

She drew deeply on the cigarette and waved a hand toward the empty chair. Blowing smoke away from him, she surveyed Ryan from the corner of her eye.

"Is this your hangout?"

He sat, rolling a beer bottle between the palms of his hands. "Not really. I come once or twice a month. Maybe. They have really good nachos. Plate this big," he indicated holding his hands apart, "and loaded with everything. When I want good nachos, this is where I come."

"I'll remember that." She grinned, squinting through the smoke. "Good nachos are hard to find." She looked around. "Is your wife here? Who did you marry? Someone a year or so behind my class, wasn't it?"

He chugged on the beer and nodded as he swallowed. "Amanda Morrison. We divorced almost twenty years ago.

"Wow. Time flies. Didn't you ever remarry?"

He shook his head. "Nah. It wasn't a good experience, and I was real bitter for awhile. You still married to…anyone?"

She rolled her head from side to side, eyes closed, and lips clenched. "Nobody. I tried it three times and only liked it once. He died. Not bitter though. Just wasn't right for me."

"Kids?"

She wished he wouldn't ask her personal questions. "Seven, counting his, mine, and ours."

His eyes widened and he whistled. "No kidding! Seven?"

She smiled and took another cigarette from the case. "I had two with my first husband. My second husband had three when I married him, and I had a set of twins with Mr. Three. What about you?"

"One daughter. After the divorce, Amanda did everything she could to poison Heather against me. But we have a pretty good relationship now. She's twenty-six and living in California. Don't you know those things will kill you?"

"What things?"

He took the cigarette from her and smashed it in the ashtray.

"Hey!"

He grinned at her. "How about a dance? I remember you could really cut a rug."

"Cut a rug?" She stared at him in amazement. "Cut a rug? You actually said that?"

Still grinning, he grabbed her hand and pulled her on the dance floor. "My dad used to always say that."

"Well, yeah. Cut a rug. That's from your dad's generation. Not ours."

He twirled her and then pulled her back to him. "Okay, smarty pants, what should our generation say?"

She enjoyed herself and that surprised and frightened her. After the music ended Ryan led her to a booth where he ordered nachos and two beers. They sat across from each other, eating and drinking and talking about the past. Karen told him about the reunion and the purpose behind it. He told her about his contracting business. They discussed family and friends and what they had done in the last thirty years. When closing time came, Ryan escorted her to her car.

"I've enjoyed seeing you, Karen. Do you suppose there would be time in your busy week to get together again?"

She fiddled with the keys before looking back at him. Her smile was a little sad, a lot regretful.

"I don't know, Ryan. This week was planned over thirty years ago, and I owe it to the girls to spend as much time with them as I can. Besides, in a week, I'll be out of here again, and I don't know when I'll ever return."

His smile faded a little, but his voice was firm. "All the more reason to see you again while I've got the chance." He dug a card out of his pocket and handed it to her. "This has my home, office, and cell phone numbers. Give me a call if you get hungry for nachos."

She took the card and read, "Ryan Wardlow, Contractor."

Nodding, she tucked the card in her purse.

"Thanks. It really has been good seeing you. You know, I

always hoped you would ask me out, and you never did. Now you're asking, and I can't go. Why didn't you ask when we were in high school? I mean, if you don't mind telling me."

He snorted and laughed. "Your six older brothers, that's why! Because I was a hotshot football and basketball player, they seemed to think I was dangerous for their little sister. I was as innocent as they came."

"Sure you were," she said. "Well, good night."

He nodded and backed away from the car so she could drive away.

She had had such a crush on Ryan Wardlow in her freshman year. Now she had had a very pleasant few hours with him. But she didn't dare get too close. There were things he didn't know. Things that would make him run so fast, he wouldn't even take time to look back.

If only she had been wiser, stronger. If only she didn't have the heavy burden that would repulse not only Ryan but Annette, Stacy, and Paula as well. If only she were as intelligent and sophisticated and suave as everyone seemed to think she was.

If only she didn't have a prison sentence threatening her every day.

Chapter 9

Irene

Paula picked up Stacy and they arrived at the Family Diner and Truck Stop the same time as Annette and Karen did, each in their own vehicles. Once seated, they studied the menu with the same determination they used to study their history and chemistry notes.

"This is a nice place," Paula said. "Bonnetville needed something like this. I wonder how long it's been here."

Stacy folded her menu and set it aside. "I'm pretty sure Nina told me they just celebrated the tenth anniversary. Can you believe it? I wish they had had a place like this when we lived here."

Karen added her menu to Stacy's. "All we had was that little hamburger joint across the street from the school and that one dinky diner on Main Street. What was the name of that place?"

"Dinky Diner," the other three chorused.

"Right." She looked at the waitress who arrived with pen and pad. "Two eggs, sunny-side up. Bacon, crisp. Hash browns. Toast, whole wheat. Orange juice and coffee. Lots of coffee." Karen sat back with a grin. "The coffee can start any time."

Annette ordered a bagel with cream cheese, two slices of bacon, and a fruit cup. Stacy chose blueberry pancakes with sausage, and Paula ordered the Western Omelet. They settled back to enjoy a cup of coffee as they waited for the meal to arrive.

"Did everyone have a good evening?" Paula asked.

"So-so," Annette said. "I called Brent and then read until I fell asleep. How about you?"

Paula shrugged. "I tried to read, but I guess I was too keyed up."

"Me, too," Karen said. "I went for a drive. What did you do, Stace?"

Stacy set her cup back in the saucer and patted her mouth with a paper napkin.

"I called Daniel, and I visited with Nina for awhile. What is everyone going to do after we see Davis at the bank?"

Annette and Karen exchanged grins.

"Anybody want to run to Hazelwood for some shopping?" Annette moved her cup aside so the waitress could set down her plate.

"Hazelwood? Isn't that like an hour away?" Paula smiled her thanks to the waitress.

"So? You got anything better to do?" Karen gave her that challenging stare that used to start so much bickering.

But Paula refused to bite. Instead, she shrugged and cut into her omelet.

"I have no objections to going," she said. "But I know Stacy is having a family dinner tonight, so we need to be back early enough so that she can get ready for that."

Stacy nodded. "Nina's brother and sister are coming. They live in Cullen. I didn't know if anyone had any special plans, but I hated to disappoint them."

"I too have a dinner engagement," Annette said. "So we'll be back early. I've been invited to dinner at the mayor's house." She waved her fork loftily and faked a pompous air. "A political thing, I'm sure. But he said something about barbecued spare ribs, so there are benefits."

The food was good, and they ate with a gusto not normally enjoyed by women constantly watching their diet and figures. When they finished, they settled back for a final cup of coffee.

"Who is that woman over there?" Stacy whispered and nodded discreetly toward the counter. "She looks so familiar, but I can't place her. Don't look, Karen! I don't want her to think we're talking about her."

"We are talking about her. At least, you are." Karen gave her a wicked grin and took a compact out of her purse, angling the mirror just right so that she could see the woman. "Humm. I think we should know her, but I just can't--"

"I wonder if she's been sick," Paula said. "I know a lot of women wear turbans, but she seems awfully pale, too."

The woman suddenly walked in their direction.

"Uh, oh, Paula, you must have offended her. She's coming over to kick your butt."

"Karen, quit teasing!" Stacy smiled as the woman stopped at

their table.

"Y'all don't remember me, do you?" she said.

The four of them exchanged looks.

"Actually," Annette said, "we do recognize you. But we can't come up with a name. Help us out, will you?"

The woman's smile was pretty but strained. "Irene. Crawford. Used to be Irene Miller. I married--"

"Mark Crawford!" Karen pounded the table. "Of course! How are you, Irene?"

Paula pulled a chair over from another table and gestured for Irene to join them. Irene sat down with a sigh.

"Thanks. I can only stay a moment. My sister owns the restaurant here. She does most of the cooking. You remember Laura? She was five years behind us in school."

"Oh, I remember! She was a friend of my sister Jana Sue," Paula said. "Tell her the omelet was delicious. Just the way I like it."

"I'll tell her."

"So, Irene have you stayed here in Bonnetville?" Annette asked.

Irene nodded. "Yeah. Mark and I married a couple years out of high school. We got five kids, all grown now. I got six grandkids with the seventh on the way."

"Really!" Stacy smiled at her. "And you're not even showing pictures?"

Irene's smile was easier now. "I left my purse in the car. But you better watch it the next time I see you!"

"We'd love to see pictures," Paula said. "How is Mark?"

Irene grimaced. "He's okay. Been working too hard. He runs the septic company in town."

"That sounds like job security," Karen said. "Doesn't he have anyone working for him? I mean, so he doesn't have to work so hard."

Irene swallowed and glanced out toward the parking lot. "Well, he did have. But he had to let Jules go because we needed the money we could save by not paying out a salary. You see, I've been sick. We got insurance. Some. But it's never enough."

"Oh, Irene, I'm so sorry." Tears filled Stacy's eyes. She had always been the gentle, soft-hearted one. "I hope you're better now."

Irene tried to smile but couldn't quite pull it off. She shrugged instead.

"Can we help in any way?" Annette was the constant politician.

Irene shook her head. "Cancer. I had a double mastectomy, and I'm still going through chemo. It's rough, and it's expensive. I feel bad. We've used up most of our savings. The insurance has about paid the max. I work when I can. I clean the bank and a few little businesses. Mark takes over that, too, when I'm too sick to do it. The kids help. They all live in the area. All five of them." The pride glistened in her eyes. "I have really good kids. Y'all got kids?"

"Yes." Annette smiled. "I have two. Stacy has one and a couple of stepchildren, too. Paula has three. And Karen has you beat. She has seven."

"Seven!" Irene stared in disbelief. "You, Karen? Aren't you the one who always said you didn't want anything to get in your way of life and fun?"

Karen reached for her coffee cup, but it was empty. "Well, I grew up some. Found out that kids can be life and fun. Besides, I didn't have them all! I had four of them. The other three came with a marriage. At some point and time, we all have to grow up."

"Speaking of time," Paula said, "we will be late if we don't get going. I'm so glad we got to see you, Irene. We'll be praying for you. It will be better soon, I know."

One by one, the four gave Irene a hug and words of encouragement. When they left, she was dabbing her eyes with a napkin.

"How blessed I feel at this moment," Paula said once they all piled in Annette's SUV. "Please, don't let me gripe or complain even once this week. I really have too much to be grateful for."

"Me, too," Stacy said.

Annette buckled her seat belt. "Poor Irene. Cancer is such a brutal illness. I hope she's getting good care."

"Remember how she used to try and hang out with us?" Karen said. "And we always managed to shake her off?"

"Some things I try to forget," Annette said.

Chapter 10

Meeting with Davis

He felt shabby just standing next to them, and he wasn't any slouch himself. He worked out a couple time a week and played tennis and softball. He had weathered the years well. But these four – the Fearless Foursome – looked incredible. Peggy would be jealous if she saw them. Happily, she was in New York visiting their daughter.

"Ladies," he said and waved to a semi-circle of chairs he had placed in front of his desk. "Could I offer you some coffee?"

"Whatcha got in chocolate?" Karen asked.

His face reflected dismay and all four of the women laughed.

"Ignore her, Davy," Annette said. "We just had a huge breakfast at the Family Diner. We couldn't eat another bite."

"But for future reference," Karen said, a playful warning in her voice.

He grinned. Damn, she had him again. Karen always had had a way. He sat in the chair behind his desk and leaned back to look at them.

He had enjoyed all four of them for different reasons. Stacy, so gentle and kind-hearted, had brought out the macho in him. He longed to protect her. It was something of a status symbol to walk around holding hands with Stacy Winters. All the guys wanted to date her just because she was sweet and innocent and she made them feel strong and important.

Annette was another story. She was tough and quick. No one could ever put anything past her. She was ambitious and determined, and they were too much alike to be a couple. But he liked Annette because she was decent and honest and a challenge.

Karen was a pistol. Having six older brothers had taught her to take care of herself. Just knowing about those brothers kept all the boys in line. Karen was fun and daring. But she didn't like anyone trying to rule over her. She was too much of a challenge for Davis Griffin who liked to be the dominant partner in a relationship. Funny that he should have married Peggy. Davis didn't feel like he had had the final word in anything in all the years of his marriage.

Now Paula was the girl friend he had had the longest. He remembered dating her from the beginning of their junior year through Christmas. Paula was the one he would have liked to go all the way with. But she was so afraid of the chaste upbringing she had had. And being poorer than the other three girls made Paula self-conscious and hesitant to be her own person. She relied on the leadership of the other three, particularly Annette and Karen. Davis could understand that intimidation. He came from the richest family in town, and his wife and daughter made him feel inferior in almost every way. He didn't feel bullied exactly but he sure didn't feel like he had the respect he needed.

"Would it help if we took off our clothes?"

Davis jumped. His face burned as he managed a weak grin.

"Karen!" Stacy chided her friend. "Leave him alone. He's probably overwhelmed with the four of us barging in on him."

"We had an appointment," Annette said. She watched him, the mischief dancing from her sapphire colored eyes. "Do we scare you, Davy? It was hard for you to manage us one at a time. Do you feel like we're gaining up on you?"

Davis gave a loud laugh and slapped the desk. Damn, if they weren't the same ornery, impish girls they had been thirty years ago.

"I'm just thinking that I would be the envy of our entire senior class. Here I am sitting with the four best looking and smartest girls of the entire group, and there's no one to see me. Where's the justice in that?"

"I'm sure you can do a good job of describing it all," Paula said. "How many do you think will show up for the homecoming?"

The talk shifted to families and old times and "remember when". Downstairs, the bank closed and still they talked. Finally, Karen turned the discussion to the reason they were there.

"We'll chitchat more later, Davis. Right now, we need to be sure everything is ready for you to give us a check next Saturday. Any problems there?"

"None whatsoever," he assured them. "Just give me the name,

and I can have the check ready in ten minutes."

"We don't have the name yet," Annette said. "But we will next Saturday. Can we set a time? Would 11:00 be okay?"

Davis jotted the time down on his daily calendar and nodded. "Eleven will be fine. There's no stipulations? You want a check and not cash or traveler's checks?"

"A check," Annette confirmed. "Have it made out, and we'll give you the name then. Okay-dokey?"

"Okay-dokey."

The four women stood in unison. Davis rose to his fee, wishing he could prolong the get-together.

"I…will we be seeing you this week? I mean, there are some functions going on before the game and dance next Saturday."

"We'll see you around," Karen assured him. "But right now, we're headed to Hazelwood for some heavy duty shopping."

One by one, they either shook Davis's hand or gave him a quick hug. He watched them from the office window as they all got into an SUV driven by Annette. He sighed. They had put on a little weight, which they needed to do. There were some lines around the eyes and mouth and a few gray hairs. But they were the same smart mouths and teases they had been thirty years ago.

Gosh, it had been good to see them.

Chapter 11

Shopping

Paula checked her cash while pretending to try on a blouse in the dressing room. She had such limited funds that she couldn't even enjoy the shopping spree. Gary had cheated her out of her fair share of their finances especially since the law did not require him to pay alimony. Some investments they had made wouldn't pay off for another eight years, and Gary had liquidated all other mutual assets that had given her a little. That money had to last as long as possible. She was trying hard to make it as a writer, but it was more difficult than she had expected it to be. Two children's books, although moderately successful, did not pay the bills.

She lived frugally and would have regardless of her financial situation. It was the way she was raised. Her apartment in Amarillo would be considered shabby by a lot of people, but it suited her fine. It was actually a garage apartment located at the back of an elderly man's house. She paid a modest $300 a month for the three rooms and bath. In exchange for the low rent, she checked on Mr. Douglas when his daughter was away and drove him to doctor's appointments, for groceries, and to his weekly potluck and games day at the senior citizens center.

Paula would have liked a new pantsuit to wear to the game and dance Saturday night, but it had not been in her budget. She had bought only one new dress since her divorce two years before. That dress was a celebration as she appeared on her first talk show after her book *A Person for Puppy* came out. Since it was a basic navy blue, she had been able to change its appearance with scarves, jackets, and jewelry. At home she wore faded jeans and shirts.

The other three didn't seem to have any restrictions to prevent them from enjoying the day. Annette chose dresses, pantsuits, jeans, and shirts like she was buying for all of them and their families. Karen tried on one outfit after another, but was very selective in her choices. She didn't however, Paula noticed, pay much attention to the price tags.

Even Stacy seemed to be having a good time though she wasn't buying much for herself. She choose a number of items for her husband and son and then added other things for her stepdaughters and their children. Paula pretended to encourage them and share in the fun. But deep down, she wished she had stayed in the cozy little cottage behind her brother's house. Checking her watch, Paula realized she could call a special friend and probably catch him for a change. But she didn't want to do that within sight and sound of her friends. They would misinterpret things, and Paula was having enough trouble keeping the proper perspective without their wisecracks and nosy meddling. She knew she should not make the call, but she felt the need. She loved the other three dearly, but she felt so out of place in their presence.

Idly, she took outfits off the rack, examined them, and hung them back up. She was about to do that again, when she paused to really examine what she was holding. It was an orchid colored velour pantsuit with a soft turtleneck that almost called her name. She peeked at the price tag, hoping it might possibly be in her range. The cost made her gasp, and she hastily shoved it back on the rack. Without looking back, she marched off and decided to wait for the others in the shoe section where she could sit down.

Karen watched Paula. Once Paula walked away, Karen slipped over and covertly looked at the garment. It was pretty and just the style that would look good on Paula. The price tag said, "89.95." Karen grimaced. Of course, that was too steep for Paula. Of the four of them, only Annette would buy it without hesitation. Still…Paula hadn't bought a thing, and Karen wisely guessed that her friend didn't buy much that wasn't necessary.

Making sure Paula wasn't watching, Karen took the outfit to the cashier and held it up.

"I think this price tag is wrong. Look at this. That's a stain, isn't it? And here the seam is coming out. Where is the manager? I think ninety dollars is too much for flawed merchandize."

The cashier looked annoyed but quailed under Karen's gaze. "I'll call the manager over," she said.

Moments later an older woman examined the pantsuit.

"Well, yes, the seam does seem to be coming out. But only

here. The rest seems quite secure. And I don't think this is a stain. I can practically brush it off."

"So you're happy with an exorbitant price on an inferior garment?"

The manager started to speak, to point out that ninety dollars was hardly an outrageous cost, but changed her mind. She snatched up a marking pen and slashed through the "89.95. "I guess we can mark it down a bit. Let's see. Ten dollars off seems fair, don't you think?"

"I don't think. Someone will need to mend it. And it will have to be cleaned before it can be worn."

"It's washable. Very easy to care for," the manager said.

"I doubt it is worth more than forty dollars," Karen persisted. "At the very most."

"Then I suggest you look for another item. This probably isn't what you're wanting."

Karen glanced over her shoulder and saw that Paula was talking on her cell phone. The expression n Paula's face almost made Karen forget the saleslady. It was curious how animated Paula had suddenly become.

"Listen, you see that lady over there? I'm going to have her try this outfit on. If she likes it, I want her to have it. But she's had some setbacks lately. Lousy bum of an ex-husband, if you know what I mean. She deserves a treat, but she won't break down and buy it if it's too expensive. I want you to mark this down to $40. If she seems to like the suit but still hesitates to buy it, knock off whatever it takes. I'll pay the difference when she isn't looking."

"Oh." The manager watched the woman talking on the cell phone. She was dressed in a faded pair of jeans with a bright red blouse. She could certainly use a nice outfit. "All right," the manager agreed. She slashed through the price tag and wrote "$39.99" in bold red letters. "I really can't go any lower." She sounded apologetic now rather than miffed.

"Thanks." Karen smiled her gratitude. "I'll settle with you when I pay for my things."

Taking care that Paula wasn't watching, Karen approached Stacy with the outfit in hand.

"Stace, I want you to show this to Paula and insist she try it on. It's pretty. It would look great on her, and she deserves something new."

Stacy checked the price tag. "I don't think Paula has much money, Karen. Why don't we just buy it for her?"

Karen shook her head. "I thought of that. She'd never go for it. That stupid pride of hers. Just take it to her and tell her you spotted it and know it would look fantastic on her."

Stacy hesitated and watched Paula put her phone back in her purse. "But why make her feel bad, Karen? She won't buy it. I know she won't."

"Oh, for Pete's sake!" Karen snatched the suit away from Stacy. "I'll do it myself."

"Never mind." Stacy took the garment back, smoothed it on the hanger, and walked to Paula.

"Paula, look at this! It's beautiful! And it would look great on you. Why don't you try it on?"

Paula's eyes widened as she recognized the very outfit she had rejected just minutes earlier.

"I know. I love it. But…it's a little expensive, Stacy. And I really don't need it."

Stacy checked the price tag as though she hadn't seen it before.

"It's ninety dollars, Stacy."

"No, it isn't. It's marked down to forty."

"What!" Paula stood and looked at the tag. "But I just…wow. It is forty. That's a fair price. But I just checked it and it was ninety dollars. I'm sure of it."

"Oh, I can explain that," said the manager who was walking by. "A customer pointed out a tiny place here where the seam is coming out. And there is a smidgen of dirt here on the sleeve. So it's marked down though I don't think they are major problems."

"No," Paula said thoughtfully. "Easily fixed. But…well, I guess it wouldn't hurt to try it on."

"Great!" Stacy said. "Go ahead. And come out here and show us."

Paula loved the way the fabric caressed her skin. The color was very flattering with her dark hair and green eyes. And best of it, it had a slimming effect that really pleased her. But forty dollars! She was used to spending Wall-Mart prices where she could get three pair of jeans for that price.

"Get out here, Lowe," Karen called. "Strut your stuff, baby."

Paula walked out slowly and turned for their review.

"Oh, Paula," Stacy said. "It's gorgeous! It's you! You've got to get it."

"I don't know." Paula's voice was scarcely more than a whisper.

"Wow, Paula." Annette walked up, her arms full of items. "That's you! You're going to get it, aren't you?"

"She is," Karen said. "You're got to, Paula. You'll show us all up if you wear it on Saturday. But I'm willing to risk it."

Paula turned before the mirror, examining herself from every angle.

"I don't know. I mean, it is a good price. I...I guess I really didn't bring anything to wear to the game and dance. I haven't bought anything in awhile, so maybe--"

"If you don't get it I will," Karen said. "I can wear that purple color, too."

Paula preened. "Forget it! This color won't work for you. Especially with that red hair. I better buy it just to keep you from making an idiot of yourself."

Karen hissed. "I can wear anything I want and look terrific."

"Not this," Paula sang out as she disappeared into the dressing room.

Stacy and Karen exchanged grins. Annette caught their looks and understood at once.

"You two should be ashamed of yourselves," she whispered. "Maybe she can't afford to buy it."

"She can't, but she needs to," Karen said. "It will make her feel good."

On the way back to Bonnetville, Annette and Karen kept up a steady conversation in the front seat. Stacy anchored herself in a corner and dozed. Paula took out a purse size sewing kit and mended the seam, a look of ecstasy on her face.

Chapter 12

Karen's Dad

Annette dropped Stacy off at her niece's house and then left Karen and Paula at the Family Diner and Truck Stop. She gave a honk and a wave as she sped off to get ready for dinner with the mayor.

Paula couldn't resist another look in the bag. The pantsuit felt so soft and the color was so pretty. How could she have passed up such a buy?

Karen hid a smile. If Paula had refused to buy the darn suit, she would have bought it and left it in Paula's car. Every woman deserved a new outfit once in awhile.

Paula put the bag on her car seat and turned back to Karen.

"So how are you spending the evening?"

Karen shrugged. "I thought I might go to the nursing home. See my dad."

Paula's mouth flew open. "I'm sorry," she said. "I didn't realize he was still alive. Oh! That sounded--"

Karen fluttered a hand in dismissal.

"I haven't seen him in a few years. He was pretty bad then, and I understand he's worse now. He won't even know me, but…well, duty calls and all that."

"But you love your dad. You were always so close," Paula said. "I envied you that."

"Times changed."

Paula waited for Karen to explain, but her friend just twisted the car keys and stared in to the distance.

"Can I come with you?" Paula asked.

Karen looked up, her eyes wide.

"You mean it?"

"Absolutely. Hop in."

"No, we'll take my car."

Karen unlocked both front doors and slid behind the wheel. Paula hesitated a moment and then reached for the plastic bag she had put in her car.

Karen hooted with laughter.

"You think somebody is going to steal your clothes?"

"No," Paula said as she got in the car. She slipped the bag on the floor between her feet. "Because I'm going to have them with me!"

Paula couldn't believe she didn't recognize Mr. Montgomery. Always such a big man with a powerful stance and aggressive attitude, he had withered down to skin and bones. The shell of a man she had once admired hardly noticed their presence.

"Hi, Dad." Karen knelt before her father who huddled in a wheelchair. A red plaid blanket covered his knees. Karen pulled it down over his legs and gently tucked it in.

"Hello, Mr. Montgomery." Paula thought she should say something more. Then she thought she shouldn't say anything. She settled herself in a chair a few feet away.

"How are you, Dad? Are you happy here?"

He stared at a spot on the blanket.

"Do they treat you well, Dad? Have any of the boys been to see you?"

He mumbled and Karen moved closer to him.

"Do you need anything, Dad? Do you know who I am? It's me. Karen. Your little Princess." Karen's voice cracked and she ducked her head. Paula looked away, blinking back tears.

Mr. Montgomery mumbled again and Karen took his hands in hers.

"What is it, Dad?"

"Princess," he said.

"Yes! It's me, Dad."

"Had my pretty Princess."

"I'm still here."

He shook his head. "Princess...gone."

Karen's features distorted as she tried to deal with this. Paula pressed a hand to her mouth and let the tears trickle. She was thankful neither of her parents had had to grow old in a nursing home with no one close to love them. But they would have had someone. She, William, and Jana Sue would never have abandoned their parents. Never.

"Dad, I--"

"Pretty girl."

"Dad--"

"Don't know where she went."

"I just…I got married. I…I had kids. I--"

"Loved her so much. She went bad. Don't know why."

"No! Dad--"

"Didn't love me anymore."

"That's not true! You told me to go away!" Tears streamed down Karen's face, her mascara leaving black streaks.

Paula could stand it no longer. She joined Karen and put a hand on Mr. Montgomery's knee.

"Mr. Montgomery, I know your daughter very well. Karen is a loving, wonderful person. She loves you so much, and you can be proud of her."

He frowned, cocking his head to one side much like a dog questioning his master.

"Karen? Kari-Barri?"

A sob escaped Karen as she heard another of her father's pet terms for the first time in decades.

"Where's my Karri-Barri? Where's my Princess?"

"Right here, Dad." Karen pressed his hands to her face. "I'm right here, Daddy."

He pulled away from her. "No! No! Where's my little girl?

Where--"

"Daddy! Daddy, I'm right here."

An aide rushed over and put a hand on the old man's shoulder.

"He's getting agitated. Means he's tired. I better put him to bed. Why don't you come back during the day? He's usually calmer then."

Karen nodded, unable to speak. Paula longed to put an arm around her friend but knew Karen would resent it. They walked to the car without speaking.

It wasn't until they got back to Paula's car that Karen broke the silence.

"Don't forget that bag. I don't want you waking me up at midnight looking for the thing."

Paula gathered up the bag and her purse.

"Do you...should we get supper while we're here?"

Karen shook her head. "I'm not hungry. Do you want something? They probably have take-out if you don't want to stay and eat alone."

Paula shook her head. "No. I think I'll just go back to William's and call it a day. I'm feeling tired."

"Me, too. See you tomorrow."

Karen put the car in gear and drove quickly out of the parking lot. Paula hadn't even had time to unlock her door before Karen pulled back and stopped, spraying gravel.

"By the way, I just wanted to say thanks. You know."

Paula nodded. "Don't be upset. He doesn't know what he's

saying."

Karen stiffened and she clenched her mouth tightly before finally speaking. "He may not know what's he saying, but he definitely knows what he's feeling. Later."

William's house was dark, and so was the backyard path to her little cottage. Paula found a small flashlight in her purse and used it to find the keyhole in the door. Once inside, she carefully hung the pantsuit on a plastic hanger and then propped the pillows up on the bed and leaned against them.

Today had been taxing for a number of reasons. But watching Karen with her father almost had been more than she could stand. Is that how she would end up? Alone with no one to care?

She broke down and cried hard, deep soul-wrenching sobs that left her drained and depressed. She reached for her purse and pulled out the cell phone. Should she call him? No, she shouldn't. She shouldn't allow herself to care even a little bit. Almost against her will, she punched in the numbers and waited while the phone rang. When he answered she almost cried out in relief and a desire to be with him.

"Hi!" Even to herself her voice was forced and strained.

It didn't fool the party on the other end.

"No, I'm okay. Really. Well, something did happen with my friend Karen today. It was pretty upsetting. You're sure you don't mind my telling you? I know you do. Thank you. That means so much. Okay, here goes. We went to the nursing home to see

Karen's father. It was just so sad. So sad."

Karen stepped out of the shower and rubbed herself dry. She had tried to wash away every sin, every disappointing act she had ever committed. But she felt as dirty and as much a failure as she had before turning on the water.

She wasn't a bad person. She wasn't! She had just made some bad choices. But she had learned from her mistakes and experiences. Shouldn't that count for something? She lay nude on the bed, too exhausted to even put on the red nightgown she had brought. When the phone rang by her bed, she thought about not answering it. But afraid that the caller would decide to come and check on her, she reached for the phone.

"Yeah? Oh! Hi, Ryan. Yes, I'm fine. You're where? Yes, I suppose a piece of pecan pie and a cup of coffee would be good. Well…so long as you're buying! Give me ten minutes and I'll meet you in the restaurant. Make that twenty minutes. Go ahead and eat. I'll join you for dessert."

Renewed, she reached for a clean pair of jeans and a knit top. Better that she should be with company tonight rather than being lonely and depressed in her room. And at the moment, she couldn't think of any better company than Ryan Wardlow.

Chapter 13

The Time Gets Closer

Paula locked the restroom door in the church and counted her money. William and Claire had hinted during the drive to the church that they were really going to need the cottage for the upcoming weekend after all. To their surprise and delight, both their college age son and daughter would be coming and bringing three or four friends each. There was simply no room in the house for all of them.

She sighed. She didn't know if she would be able to get a room now with Homecoming weekend coming up. But she supposed she had better try. She took out two hundred dollars and stuck it between a picture of her children and one of her parents. That left her a hundred and fifty to get through the week.

She heard the prelude music playing, but she still took out a cell phone and punched in a number. He sounded sleepy, and she realized she must have awoken him. After all, California was two hours earlier. She apologized and explained that she might be switching living quarters soon. He was indignant. Hadn't her brother offered her the use of the cottage for the whole week? She assured him that she would be just as happy in a motel. She didn't mention that she might not be able to get a room now. And even is she did, she wasn't sure how she could afford it. Even the little dumpy Sleep-Ease on the edge of town had a "No Vacancy" sign lit up. Realizing that she should not have troubled him, she bid a hasty good-bye.

"The music is playing. I need to get in and get seated before the prayer. I just thought I would--"

She refused to say, "I just wanted to hear your voice."

"I better run. Go back to sleep. I'll talk to you again soon."

She hung up even as she heard him say, "Paula, wait! I...Paula!"

Why couldn't she just leave him alone? It was for his own good. Hers, too.

She slipped in next to her sister-in-law Claire and smiled across the aisle at Stacy who sat with her niece and family. This was just like the old days. Paula and her family sitting together; Stacy and her family together. Paula was sure that Annette and Karen would be sitting together in the Baptist Church.

They had all decided that this would be a family day. Annette and Paula would spend the day with their brothers. Stacy would be with her niece and other family members who drove in to join them. Karen declined invitations from all three friends saying she really wanted a day to drive around on her own.

After Church, William and Claire, along with their youngest son

Rob, drove to Wendy's.

"This is our weekly routine," Claire told her. "Oh, once in awhile we'll make it to Taco Bell or pizza. But we save the nice restaurants for special occasions."

Over burgers and chicken strips and fries, they discussed family and all the changes in Bonnetville. Then Claire directed the topic back to the upcoming weekend.

"I wonder if maybe we could rent a camp bed or something and put in the cottage with you, Paula. Maybe you and Rob could--"

"Mom!" At seventeen, Rob would not like being stuck with his aunt.

Paula's cell phone gave the peculiar ring that signaled a missed call. She excused herself and punched in the proper numbers. The message warmed her heart.

"Hi, babe. I wish you hadn't hung up so fast. I wanted to tell you that I will be flying to Alaska this morning for a few days. We'll be checking out a possible location. Listen, I don't like the idea of your brother kicking you out. So I made a reservation for you at the Leisure Inn. I guess that is about the only place in town. Anyway, you can pick up the keys at noon on Tuesday. The reservation is through Saturday night. It's paid for and don't get all huffy with me about it. I'll be in some remote area, so I don't think there will be phone service. I'll get in touch with you later in the week. Love you, babe."

Paula folded the phone and dropped it back in her purse. She was blushing at how easy his affections were expressed. She was relieved that living quarters were resolved. She was touched that he had taken the initiative to solve her problem. And she was embarrassed and a bit annoyed that he had taken it upon himself to pay for it. But overall, she was happy to have someone take care of her even from a distance.

"Relax, Rob," she said. "You can keep your room. I have reservations at the Leisure Inn on Tuesday. You won't need the cottage any sooner than that, will you, William?"

Her brother blinked and reddened. "No, sis, of course not. The kids won't be in until Friday actually. I mean, I don't want you to leave. We're not kicking you out, you know. We're just trying to figure out--"

She waved a hand at him, feigning a nonchalance she didn't feel. "It's taken care of, everything's settled. I was wondering though if you would mind if I invited the girls over tomorrow afternoon for a cookout. I saw that wonderful grill you built." The idea had just come to her, but she was pleased with it.

William and Claire were exuberant in offering her whatever she needed.

"We're on a bowling league in Cullen on Monday evenings," William said. "And Rob always spends the night with a friend. So you ladies would be on your own. We don't get in until 11:00, so there would be no one to disturb you."

"Thanks," Paula said. And she meant it. She was a little giddy and lighthearted and bore no ill-will toward anyone. Well, maybe her ex. Just a little. Maybe she would reach a point where the thought of him no longer bothered her, but she wasn't there yet.

By nine that evening, Paula had contacted Annette, Karen, and Stacy and they had all agreed to meet at the cottage at 2:00 the following day.

"We'll eat and drink and be merry," Karen said when Paula finally reached her. And then the next day we start our laud and applaud sessions."

"Ooo…kay," Paula said. "See you tomorrow.

Chapter 14

Catching Up

Annette, Stacy, and Karen pulled up to William's house right at 2:00 on Monday afternoon. Paula was ready for them. She had purchased small steaks and late ears of corn, made a huge salad, and baked a cheesecake and chocolate chip cookies. She had filled a small cooler borrowed from her brother with soft drinks, water, and fruit juices. She had taken advantage of Claire's insistence that she use anything in the house to prepare for her friends. Paula realized it was guilt on William's and Claire's part that made them so generous, and she could be gracious enough to accept it.

William brought lawn chairs out of the garage and cleaned them off. He promised to start the grill before he and Claire left for Cullen for their bowling night.

Paula greeted her friends. They admired the small cottage and decided to take advantage of the warm fall day by sitting outside. Claire tactfully left them alone saying she needed a nap before their evening out.

"This is nice," Karen said. She took a bite of cookie and then another one. "Hey! I didn't know you could bake. This here's the real deal."

"Are you kidding me?" Paula laughed. "Baking was what I did the majority of the years I was married. Wait until you try my cheesecake!"

"Before we get too fat and drowsy," Annette said, "I'd like to make some proposals."

"Proposals?" Karen asked sending a suspicious look toward Annette.

Annette laughed and held up a restraining hand. "Okay, how about suggestions? Do you like that word better?"

"Depends," Karen said. "Does it involve me?"

"Of course, it involves you. It involves all of us. It has to do with why we are here this week."

"Oh, that." Karen sipped her cola and reached for another cookie. "Suggest away then."

"Thank you." Annette smiled at her friends. "If you remember, our original plan was to award the money to the one who had contributed the most to society. Right?" She continued after they all nodded. "Part of achieving was also the failing. I'm sure we've all had some of that along the way. How we failed, and more importantly, how we handled that failure plays a part in what we achieved."

"So what are you saying?" Paula asked. Her frown and hesitancy indicated that airing her dirty laundry was not part of what she hoped to be doing.

"Don't worry." Annette was quick to reassure them. "I'm not

suggesting we confess our every sin, though I can tell you that I would think no less of either of you. I'm saying that we're not perfect. That imperfection is an indication of our success. We achieved in spite of, or maybe because of our failures or weaknesses. Oh, brother! I'm not stating this well at all."

Obviously, she wasn't as the other three regarded her with everything from derision to distrust.

"Okay, forget it. I just thought--"

"I guess I don't mind," Paula said. "I think you all know my failures anyway."

Annette shrugged. "Just present yourselves any way you're comfortable. I thought I had it well thought out and planned, but apparently my mind sees better than my mouth speaks. I need to remember that when Brent makes his campaign speeches."

"So he is running!" Stacy's squeal brought laughter from Karen and Paula awhile Annette blushed deep red.

"Oh, good grief! I wasn't supposed to say anything. What an idiot I am!" Annette chided herself and put both hands to her face. "Please, please, please keep this to yourselves. Brent won't trust me with another secret."

"It's great news though," Paula said. "When's he planning to announce?"

"The day after Thanksgiving," Annette said. "I know the press is already speculating, but please don't confirm anything."

"My lips are sealed," Karen said and reached for another cookie.

"They certainly are," Stacy agreed with a laugh. "Sealed with chocolate chips!"

Karen stuck a chocolate covered tongue out at her friend. "Now back to telling all our dirty little secrets."

"What? No! That's not at all what I meant!" Annette was distressed that she had presented her idea so badly. That and letting Brent's secret out put her in a very uncomfortable position. "I was going to suggest that we meet tomorrow and tell our glories. Then on Wednesday, we could explain how we achieved what we have in spite of or because of whatever obstacles we encountered. And then Thursday, I was going to suggest we tell how we would use the funds. Now that I've stuck my foot in my mouth, I think I'll keep it tightly shut."

"Wait a minute." Karen sat up, spilling her drink. "There were never any stipulations on how the funds could be used."

"Right," Paula agreed. "The plan was always for the one who had achieved the greatest contributions to society to get the money. Nothing was ever said about how it was to be spent."

"I didn't mean to indicate that there was to be any guidelines." Annette's tone was suddenly cool and politically correct. "I guess I was thinking that would also indicate worthiness but it's certainly not part of the deal. Forgive me. I was out of line."

There was an uneasy silence and then Stacy snatched up the plate of cookies and shoved them under Annette's nose.

"It's not your fault," she said. "You haven't had enough chocolate."

They laughed as Annette pulled away from the plate, a chocolate chip smudge on the tip of her nose.

The afternoon wore on and William started the grill as he promised. The steaks and salad and corn were devoured like they were hungry teenagers rather than middle-aged women who watched their diets. After eating and cleaning up, they settled back in the chairs to relax and let the food digest.

"Personally," Paula said, "I'd like to hear what everyone has been up to the last thirty years. I want to hear about your families, where you've been, what you've been doing."

"So would I," Stacy said. "We have so much to catch up on. I for one am ashamed that I haven't been better at keeping in touch. Paula, you're the one who is so good at that. Let's do talk about our lives. I want you to know my family, and I want to get to know each of yours."

Paula saluted her with a plastic tumbler of water.

"I'll go along with that," Karen said. "Then tomorrow I think we should start telling about our achievements. Everyone should write down everything they have accomplished. Then the next day, we should come clean and bare our souls. Then on Thursday, we can tell what we hope to do in the future. Friday and Saturday are for fun."

Annette stared at her, mouth open. "What did you just say?"

Karen grinned. "I said I think that tomorrow we should pat ourselves on the back and see who is worthy of all that money. Then we should fess up. And then we should tell how we plan to reform and go straight in the future."

"What?" Annette's voice was a high squeak.

"But right now," Karen said ignoring Annette's indignant sputters and Paula's and Stacy's laughter, "I want to hear all about Stacy's last thirty years. Take it away, girl."

Chapter 15

Stacy Leann Winters McCall Durfey

Paula brought out blankets and distributed them.

"Or would you prefer to go inside?" she asked. "If it's too cold."

"I rather stay and look at the stars," Karen said. She took a blanket and wrapped it around her. "I can't see them this clearly in Houston. Okay, Stacy, fill us in."

The others settled in lawn chairs, readjusting the head and feet rests to their comfort. Paula handed a cup of apple spice herb tea to each before settling herself as well.

Stacy sighed and looked up. "The stars are different here, aren't they? Or maybe it's just that I don't take enough time to look at them back home. But you know," she said, suddenly thoughtful, "Daniel and Austin do. They will lie on the trampoline and watch the stars for two or three hours at a time. They've invited me to join them, but I always had something else that seemed more important."

"Like laundry," Paula said.

"Or vacuuming or dishes or something equally demanding,"

Annette said. "We've all been there, done that."

"Exactly," Stacy said. "And I just this minute realized what a waste. I worried about things that don't matter one bit and missed some precious moments with my family." She covered her mouth and blinked back tears. "I miss them right now. I can hardly wait to see them on Saturday."

"All right, already," Karen said. "Start talking or we'll be here all night. You can skip the school years. I remember those."

"I don't agree," Annette said. "I'd like to hear some of your memories and impressions."

"That might be opening a can of worms," Paula said. Her voice was light, but her expression was warning. "Maybe it would be better to let bygones be bygones."

"Two clichés in one speech. And from a writer yet!" Karen shifted position and drew the blanket up under her chin.

Paula glared in her direction but quickly composed herself. "For your information, children love clichés. But anyway, I suggest we all tell what we want the way we want. Go ahead, Stacy. We're all ears."

"Three," Karen muttered.

"Give me a minute," Stacy said. Her voice was low and dreamy. "Let me get my thoughts together."

"Fine," Karen said. "Wake me when you're ready."

Stacy smiled in the darkness. They used to call Karen Miss Imp – for impatient, impetuous, and impulsive.

It she was writing her life story, would she start with her birth,

Stacy wondered. That was the reasonable thing to do. But in her mind, Stacy didn't feel like she had a lot of life until she met Daniel Douglas Durfey fourteen years ago. She had been a thirty-four year old woman, just divorced, with no hope for the future and no longing for the past. Daniel was a fifty-two year old history professor at Southern Methodist University. They had met at a Civil War presentation at the Fine Arts Center, and it had been instant like. Love had followed quickly, and they were married only three months after they met. Austin Daniel Durfey had been born fifteen months after that. The years with her husband and son were the happiest of her life. Occasionally, Daniel's two daughters from his first marriage joined them. But they were so close to Stacy's age that they seemed more like nieces than stepdaughters.

"I'm waiting," Karen said.

"I'm thinking," Stacy answered.

The first five and a half years of her life had been happy, Stacy knew. She had been cherished and babied and protected like few other little girls could ever hope to be treated. She was the unexpected baby, to say the least. Stacy's two sisters were twelve and ten years older, and her mother Nora had no thoughts of having another baby. Nora had been keenly disappointed not to have had a son, but Leland Winters was delighted to have another daughter. He loved to come home after a hard day at their service station and cuddle his little girl. Sometimes he read to her; sometimes she told him stories. When the weather was good and Leland wasn't too tired, they would take walks around the neighborhood. Leland explained things to Stacy and answered all her questions while holding her chubby little hand.

Stacy hardly knew a moment of discontent until the summer before she entered first grade. Kindergarten was not offered in all public schools at that time, and Nora Winters didn't want to spend the money necessary for private kindergarten. Besides that would necessitate driving to Cullen twice a day to take Stacy and bring her home again. Nora worked as an aide in the nursing home to bring in enough money to make ends meet. She didn't want to give up her little free time driving.

A great sadness came into their lives in July before Stacy started first grade. Leland dropped dead one evening of a heart attack while walking across the living room floor. The shock was so severe that Nora went into a depression that lasted for years. Raelene, who was eighteen at the time, gave up the college scholarship she had just been awarded at her graduation only seven weeks before and instead attended the business school in Waco. In the evenings she sat with an elderly lady to earn money. Marcy, sixteen, had taken over Stacy's care while Nora went through the motions of selling the service station and working a double shift at the nursing home in Cullen.

No one seemed to consider how losing her father, her favorite person in the world, had affected six year old Stacy. Many were the nights she had cried herself to sleep and begged someone to bring her daddy home. Entering school in the fall had proven to be a godsend as it gave Stacy an outlet she hadn't realized before.

But Stacy had had to learn to deal with other changes in life. Raelene met a soldier on leave at the movies in Cullen, and they were married and moved to an army post in Virginia. Marcy graduated from high school and went to nursing school. She eventually married a law student and moved to El Paso. For years, it was just Stacy and her mother.

On the day before she started to school, Nora decided that her children needed to go to church. She hauled her three daughters to the First United Methodist Church and marched in like it was something they did ever Sunday. Stacy was a little frightened, a little excited, and a little confused. The building was beautiful with graphic stained glass windows and an organ that made Stacy's heart thump along with the music. Stacy was particularly nervous being in Sunday school with other kids. She watched them curiously but didn't try to talk to them. In return, they ignored her, too.

But when she arrived for her first day of school, Stacy recognized a girl from the Sunday school class. They stared across the room at each other and then shyly smiled. Stacy sat in a tiny desk and the girl sat behind her. The teacher instructed them to sit quietly while she explained things to the parents. She passed out pictures of a big bear wearing a bow tie and three crayons each to keep the students busy while she took care of business. After the orientation was over and the supply list handed out, the new first graders were allowed to go home. Their first real day began the next day.

As they waited for that dismissal, Stacy got brave enough to look around. She finally faced the girl she had seen in church.

"Hi," the girl said. Then she looked down at a penny she had been twirling on her desk.

"Hi," Stacy said. "What's your name?"

The girl cocked her head to one side and examined the penny like it was from a treasure chest.

"Paula," she said finally. "What your name?"

"Stacy. I saw you yesterday."

"I saw you, too," Paula said. "I never saw you at church before though."

Stacy shrugged. "I never went before. My daddy wanted me to go, so my mama took me and my sisters. My daddy died."

Paula's eyes widened. "He did? Was he old?"

Stacy had to think about that. "I don't think so. He just fell down dead. Mama said his heart was a tack."

"Oh."

"Yeah." Stacy scratched her nose and looked around the classroom. Raelene had already taught her to count to twenty-five, and Stacy counted twenty-two other first graders.

"I'm glad my daddy didn't die," Paula said.

"I wish mine didn't either," Stacy confided. It wasn't something she could talk about with Mama or Raelene or Marcy. But she felt this girl Paula might understand.

"You can have this," Paula said and shoved the penny in Stacy's hand.

Stacy looked at the penny. Mama kept telling her how important it was to count their pennies, so it was probably a very good thing to accept any money that came along. "Okay."

The teacher reminded the students to be quiet and color their pictures. Stacy tried hard to do her best coloring. She thought it looked pretty good when it was finished. She abandoned the crayons and looked around the room again. A blond haired girl with freckles waved at her. Stacy waved and then blushed when she realized the girl wanted to borrow her blue crayon. Stacy handed it to her.

"There!" the girl said. She held up her picture for Stacy to see. "I bet my picture is the best. I know how to stay in the lines."

"It looks...pretty," Stacy said though she felt her own bear looked better.

"Yours is all scribbley," the girl said and wrinkled her nose.

Stacy was stunned at the girl's criticism. She looked at her bear and realized that it was a little drab compared to the other girl's. Stacy felt Paula looking over her shoulder.

"It looks okay," Paula said. "They both look okay. What's your name? I'm Paula. Her name is Stacy."

"Karen. I have six big brothers," she informed them. "I'm the only girl. I wish I had a sister, but my mommy said one miracle is enough. I think I'm a miracle. Do you have a sister?"

"I have two sisters," Stacy said, pride in her voice.

"Big or little?" Karen asked.

"Big. Raelene doesn't go to this school anymore. Marcy is

sixteen. She goes to a big grade. I don't have a brother. I think it would be fun to have a brother, but I don't have one."

"I have a little brother and a little sister," Paula said. "They're like babies. I'm the big sister. You are the babies in your family."

Both Karen and Stacy detected the scorn in Paula's voice and felt a little ashamed that they were babies and not the big sisters. But before they could ponder this, the teacher dismissed them with a reminder that she would see each of them at eight sharp the next morning with all the things on their supply list.

The three girls waved a shy goodbye to each other and followed their mothers out of the school. As they were instructed, they returned the next day with brand new Christmas-smelling plastic satchels, boxes of crayons, blunt scissors, paste, two fat pencils, and a big pink eraser. They felt like they had grown up tons overnight and were eager to follow this path in their school career.

Five weeks into their school year, a new girl arrived. Her name was Annette. She was a pretty dark-haired beauty who already knew how to not only recite but to write all the alphabet and count to one hundred. She could write her name neatly on lined paper and could read a few words. The entire class was in awe of her, but only Stacy, Paula, and Karen were not too intimidated to include her in their recess games. Karen felt superior the following Monday when she reported that Annette went to her church, the First Baptist.

"Well, so what?" Paula said with a sniff of disdain. "Me and

Stacy go to the Methodist Church, and that's the best one."

"It is not!" Karen answered. "The Baptist Church is. My mother said so."

Before an argument could get too heated, Stacy intervened with a challenge.

"Let's race to the swings!"

It would be only the first of many times that Stacy would waylay an argument between Paula and Karen.

The first five years of friendship had been mostly during school hours and on Sundays. In those days, families tended to stay pretty much together. Their sleepovers were cherished events, especially when it involved all four of them together. More generally, they would have only one sleeping over at a time. The parents seemed to prefer it that way.

The exception was in December when they were allowed to celebrate all their birthdays together. Paula's was the first on November 6. Stacy's was next on November 18th. Then Karen started December off with a birthday on the 2nd, and Annette's followed on the 11th. From their first year together in first grade, they had a slumber party celebrating all our birthdays, and it was the highlight of their year.

Karen faked a snore and got strangled on her own spit. The other three laughed at her sputtering and hacking.

"Serves you right, Miss Imp," Stacy said with a smile.

Karen stiffened. "What did you call me?"

Stacy blushed. Why hadn't she kept her mouth shut? She hadn't meant to bring up sore points, but Karen never had resented her nickname before.

"I'm sorry. Really, Karen. That was tactless of me. I just--"

"I haven't heard that moniker in years!" Karen laughed. "Decades! No one but you three ever called me that."

"And I had forgotten it," Annette said. "Still seems to fit though, huh, Karen?"

"Once an imp, always an imp," Karen said. "Have you got your thoughts together yet?"

"Well, if she does, she has to hold them a little longer while I go to the bathroom," Paula said. She stood and tossed the blanket aside. "I'll hurry."

"Please do," Karen said. "I'm next."

"Then me," Annette said.

Stacy relaxed, relieved that she had not offended Karen. She closed her eyes and listened to Karen and Annette chat while waiting for Paula.

The school years had been enjoyable for Stacy. She was popular with everyone, it seemed. She was usually elected for some office or other in school clubs, chosen for Homecoming Princess at the football game, and was Miss Valentine for her class most years. Lots of boys asked her out once Nora deemed her old enough to date, but her dates were closely monitored by her mother and her older sisters when they were around.

Stacy began working at the Bonnetville Bank during the fall of her junior year. She worked only on Saturday mornings, which earned her barely enough to keep her in snacks at the movies or ball games. But she worked for the whole summer between her junior and senior year and until she left for college after she graduated high school. Looking back now, that time was something Stacy didn't care to think about.

In her junior year, Nora Winters was diagnosed with kidney disease that would claim her life five years later. Once Stacy went away to college, Nora rented out the house and moved to El Paso to be close to Marcy who could take care of her. The happy, carefree days of childhood ended the moment Stacy moved to Southern Methodist University. All Nora's money went to medical expenses, so Stacy had to work and get grants and scholarships to stay in school. She often longed for those early years when her father was alive and her sisters were still home. Those were good times, and she wanted that again one day with a family of her own.

"All right, Karen, wake up," Stacy said.

"I'm awake," Karen said though her words were mumbled.

"Here goes! After graduation, I stayed here in Bonnetville and continued to work at the bank."

"Were you there when the robbery occurred?" Annette asked.

Stacy swallowed and felt herself go limp. She took a deep breath and willed herself to be calm.

"Yes, actually. Well, it was reported the day after I left, so I don't know much about it. Anyway, I left the end of August and moved to Dallas to attend SMU. I had known for awhile that I wanted to be a teacher, and I had a small scholarship. Mama had gotten sick in my junior year of high school. Kidney disease. So when I went to college, Mama rented out our house and moved to El Paso to be closer to Marcy. Marcy is a nurse, you know, and Mama felt that it would be good to have her helping make the medical decisions. Eventually Mama had to have dialysis, but it wasn't until my second year of college."

"Did you graduate from SMU?" Paula asked.

"I did. I was lucky to find an older couple with a room to rent. It had a private entrance and a private bath and was very reasonable. They liked to travel to see their kids. Then I was responsible for their two cats. It was a good arrangement. Not only that but I was hired at the day care center on campus. I worked about three hours a day so that paid my rent and gave me a little spending money. It was in my second year that I met Patrick McCall. We had a couple of classes together, and it seemed like we were always running into each other. He would sometimes visit me at the day care center and was really good with the kids. Of course, that impressed me! He wanted to be a doctor, so he was interested in my mother. He joined us in El Paso after Christmas that year."

"Yet you didn't stay married," Karen said.

"No, we didn't stay married. But we were married for several years. We married during Thanksgiving break of our junior year. We had planned to wait until summer, but Mama was declining quickly. I wanted her to be part of my wedding. And it was lovely! Not very big. Just my mother and sisters and their families and Patrick's parents, grandparents, and brother. We got married in Abilene because that was a central point for everybody. His parents paid for us to spend the night in the fanciest hotel there. I can't even remember the name of it now. But that was our honeymoon. I thought it was wonderful. We split Christmas break that year between his parents and Mama. I was shocked at how quickly she was…well, I was terrified of her dying. Patrick was a real comfort during those months. Mama fell into a coma and died the end of the following June. So she didn't live to see me graduate from college a year later. On the other hand, she also didn't live to see what a…how my marriage didn't succeed."

"Rat? Jerk? Asshole?" Karen said. "What was it you wanted to call your ex?"

Stacy giggled. "I was going to call him a dumbbell."

Karen sighed. "Of course, you were. Go on."

"As soon as we graduated from SMU, we moved to Houston so Patrick could go to medical school. I found a job teaching kindergarten and that was our life for the next eight years. I was eager to start a family, but Patrick always pointed out that we couldn't afford it. We couldn't, but since I was footing most of the bills I thought I should have a bigger say in the matter. Anyway, I stayed at the same school for eight years. I turned thirty there and began to feel that I was really missing out. Especially when I worked with those five year olds every day."

"That's because you didn't have to have them when they were two year olds," Karen said.

"Karen," Paula said, "go back to sleep. What happened then, Stacy?"

They could barely see Stacy shrug in the darkness. "Patrick graduated and was going to do his residency in Midland. But he decided that he deserved a year off. I pointed out that if anyone deserved a year off, it was me. And I definitely wanted to start a family. He then informed me that he really wasn't interested in having a family, at least not any time soon. And that he really wasn't interested in being married any longer either. I was stunned. I had worked and scrimped and tried to support him in every way. I thought maybe he was just tired and did need a break. But one evening, I decided to go to the movies while he was at the library researching some sort of horrible sounding disease. I was seated almost all the way at the top of the theater. There was a couple down the row from me who was making out big time. I was so embarrassed, I couldn't get up and walk past them. And there were no ushers around. When the movie was over and the lights came on, I almost passed out. Literally. It was Patrick and some other woman."

Stacy took a deep breath and ignored the gasps and groans from the others.

"Needless to say, that ended everything. I moved back to Dallas and got a job as a first grade teacher. I had been there a couple of years when I decided to attend a Civil War presentation at the Fine Arts Center. While I was looking over a copy of a book, a gentleman approached me and asked if I had read it. I told him I hadn't but it looked very interesting. He took the book out of my hands, wrote something inside the cover, and handed it back to me. It was Daniel Douglas Durfey, and he was the author of the book. After his lecture, we went out for a cup of coffee. It was very pleasant. I found out that he was a professor at SMU. He had been a widower for three years and had two daughters in their early twenties. It was so nice talking to him, and he was so easy to be with. I went home and read the book before I went back to school on Monday. I didn't think I would ever see him again though."

"Ah, but you did," Annette said. "When?"

"Actually, about midweek after that Friday night we met, I received a gorgeous bouquet of flowers at school with a note saying he hoped I wouldn't mind hearing from him. Mind! He called that Saturday, and we went out to eat and attended a concert in the park. It felt so right, so comfortable. We were married three months later."

"That's lovely," Paula said. "I hope I get to meet him."

"You will this weekend," Stacy said. "Anyway, he continued to teach history and I continued to teach first grade. Then in October, I found out I was pregnant. I can't tell you how thrilled I was! It was a good pregnancy, and I missed very little school. School was out on May 29, and Austin Daniel was born on the second of June. He's twelve and a half now, and the joy of our lives. He's a really good kid. Very smart. Loves astronomy and shows a talent for architecture. He plays every sport there is, I think. His older sisters, who are both old enough to be his mothers, spoil him to no end. He's only a couple of months older than the first grandchild. He has five nieces and nephews not that much younger than he is."

"Still you only have the one," Karen said. "Why didn't you have others?"

"Karen," Paula said. "That's rude."

"Oh, I don't mind telling you," Stacy said. "I had some medical problems, and it was necessary to have a hysterectomy when Austin was less than two years old. I wanted more children, but it wasn't mean to be. So I gave all my love and attention to the one. Okay, I know I've left out a lot. But the rest is for later. Who's next?"

Annette sat up. "I'll go next. But I could really use a cup of hot chocolate. Anybody else?"

"I'll get some for all of us," Paula said.

She jumped up and rushed into her brother's house so fast no one had a chance to speak.

"Humm," Karen said. "I am beginning to think that Paula would rather skip this little session of our get-together. We're not going to let her get away with that, are we?"

"Well, if she really doesn't want to," Stacy said, "maybe we shouldn't insist."

"Oh, she's going to tell her story," Annette said. "Just like the rest of us. She's had thirty years to decide what to say."

Chapter 16

Annette Kay Kimball Thackeray

Annette remembered the exact moment she met Paula, Karen, and Stacy. Her family moved to Bonnetville five weeks into the school year, and Annette had been embarrassed to enter the class when the other kids already knew each other. It didn't help that Annette's mother stood in front of the room and told Mrs. Winston that her daughter knew the entire alphabet and could write most of it. She could count to one hundred and knew several words by sight. It was true, of course. But Annette could tell that the rest of the class was not impressed. Some even seemed resentful.

At recess, kids separated into their own little groups. Annette pretended not to care that they were ignoring her. Then suddenly Karen, Stacy, and Paula appeared before her.

"We're going to take over the swings," Karen said. "Irene, Pattylyn, Donna, and Betty Jean think they're going to keep them the whole recess. But they're not. Want to help us run them off?"

Annette shrugged. "Sure," she said and wondered how they were going to achieve this feat. The other four girls seemed very comfortable and determined to hang onto the swings they had.

Annette joined the other three behind the swings.

"Remember," Karen said, "when I say 'go', start screaming like crazy."

"Okay," Paula said.

Stacy nodded. Annette gave a half shrug and waited to see what would happen.

All of a sudden, Karen said "go" and the girls screamed like demons set loose in a cemetery. Annette stared at them. The four girls on the swings twisted around to see what all the commotion was about. Betty Jean dragged her feet on the ground to stop.

Karen screamed louder and pointed to one of the swings, still soaring in the air. Paula and Stacy clutched each other. Then remembering Annette, they grabbed her arm and urged her to point, too. Annette looked and saw nothing.

"What is it?" Betty Jean said. "What's the matter with you? You crazy or something?"

"Wasps!" Karen said. She continued to pint. "There's a nest on the bottom of Pattylyn's swing. Oh, gosh! Oh, gosh. They're getting mad."

The other three swings came to quick, jerky stops and all four of the girls took off in a run, now screaming louder than Karen and her friends. Mrs. Winston looked in their direction, and Stacy gave a big wave. Karen and Paula grabbed swings and plopped on them.

"Get one, quick!" Paula said. "Hurry before they came back."

Stacy and Annette grabbed the other two swings and started

pumping with all their might. Before long, the four of them were trying to see who could get the highest. They had so much fun, they didn't hear Mrs. Winston blow the whistle signaling the end of recess. They didn't see the rest of the class line up and file back into the school. What they did hear was a severe lecture from their teacher who immediately missed part of her class and went looking for them. They were banned from the swings for the rest of the week. But from that point on, the four girls had been the closest of friends. Years later, in high school, they labeled themselves The Fearless Foursome.

Annette found school easy almost to the point of boredom, so she consistently made the highest grades. This sometimes irked Karen and Paula, who tried to compete with her. But Stacy was content to let Annette be the intellectual leader and was grateful to benefit from her tutelage.

Grades weren't the only thing they competed for either. They usually found themselves liking the same boy, tried to set the fashion each year, and tried to be the first to learn each new dance craze. But despite their competition, they wanted the glories to remain in their own tight little group. They didn't take lightly anyone else coming in first in anything.

Annette always knew she wanted to do something visible and competitive. For a long time, she thought about being a lawyer, and her parents encouraged her. But as she grew older, she was bothered by so many injustices. She decided she would rather be on the other end of the legal system – one who formed the laws and implemented them.

Annette's grades earned her a scholarship to Texas A&M University. She was determined to go there and excel as she had done all through public school. But she almost blew it the night of high school graduation.

Several in the senior class met at the little lake outside of town. It was one of the few times, Annette attended anything without at least one of her usual companions. But Stacy and Paula declined going because of family obligations, and Karen lived too far out in the other direction. Besides two of her older over-protective brothers were home from college, and they forbade her to go.

Later Annette wished someone had told her she couldn't go. But her dad, the pharmacist and one of the most respected people in town, and her mother, the nearest thing Bonnetville had to a socialite, would never have considered restricting their brainy obedient daughter. And her older brother Les really didn't care what she did so long as she kept out of his way.

Someone had managed to bring enough beer and whiskey to get the eleven students totally trashed. And that was what most of them proceeeded to do. Annette knew her parents kept liquor locked away and hidden in a hutch in the den. She had never tasted it but she was in a daring, rebellious mood.

Among the group were two of the school's few black students.

Ernie Watson was a tall, husky boy with creamy chocolate-colored skin, mischievous eyes that reminded her of the family bulldog, and a grin that lit up the night. He and Davis Griffin took turns being the star quarterback. Annette had known him for six years, but she had never really talked to him. That night she did.

Long after everyone else had staggered away, Annette and Ernie sat on the hood of Ernie's dad's old Ford and talked and drank until the bottle was empty and the night was filled with stars. Annette didn't know how it happened, but one minute they were laughing and sharing the bottle. The next moment they were in the back seat of the car with most of their clothes on the floor. It was one of those things that shouldn't have happened, wouldn't have happened if they had been sober.

It was one of the only times the class brain had been stupid.

Annette was glad the darkness hid her so well. She knew her friends, as astute as they were, would see something in her features. They would badger her until she answered their questions. And she wasn't sure she could do that even if she wanted to. Her actions over thirty years ago would now affect not only herself but Brent and the kids. She could not let that happen.

She accepted the steaming cup of hot chocolate Paula offered with a hearty laugh – too hearty for what she was feeling.

"Whipped cream! I haven't had hot chocolate with whipped cream for years!"

Paula took her own mug and sat back in the lounge chair, pulling a blanket tightly around her.

"Remember," she said, "how your dad's drug store used to

serve it with a scoop of chocolate ice cream. That was good, but it always made the hot chocolate cool off too fast. I like mine hot."

Karen slurped a big sip and shuddered. "Damn, woman! That is hot!"

"Blow on it," Paula advised. "All right, Annette, go ahead. You graduated, blah, blah, blah. Pick up from there."

Not on your life, Annette thought. But she said, "Well, I had the scholarship to A&M, so that's where I went. It was a lot tougher than Bonnetville High School, but it was worth all the work. I graduated with degrees in Business Administration and Political Science. I had discovered early that political science was my real interest, but my parents felt I needed something practical. I was fortunate in that I was immediately drawn into Texas politics. I campaigned first for our own state representative. Do you remember Earl Clausen? I helped get him in office. Then I helped send Senator Jensen to Washington. And I worked especially hard to get Governor McMillan in office. I hope you agree with me that he has been an amazing governor for the State of Texas. One of the truly dedicated politicians of our time."

"Notice she didn't mention honest," Karen said in an exaggerated stage whisper.

Stacy giggled in the dark.

"He's as honest as they come," Annette said a bit stiffly.

"For a politician." Karen's whisper was louder this time.

"Hey, wait a minute," Paula said. "You skipped some parts. Like years and years. First of all, I seem to remember you disappearing in the middle of summer after graduation. You just left with no word to any of us."

Annette was hoping they wouldn't remember that. She swallowed hard and steadied her voice.

"It was a surprise from my parents." That much was true. "I guess you could call it a late graduation present." With late being the key word. "Mother and I went on a little trip. Just the two of us."

"To the Bahamas," Stacy said with a sigh. "I've always wanted to go there. Daniel said we might when he finishes this book he's working on about the Revolutionary War."

The Bahamas. Annette hadn't wanted to say because she couldn't remember exactly where they were supposed to have gone. They had actually driven to New Orleans.

"I remember that now," Karen said. "We were all laughing because you got to go to some exotic, exciting place. And you came back pale as a ghost!"

"I was sick the whole time," Annette said. If only they knew how sick.

"So you didn't have any fun at all?" Paula asked.

"None."

Karen relaxed. "Well, I feel better. I didn't miss anything."

"Nothing." Nothing except a horror she never wanted to experience again.

"Okay, back to the story," Paula said.

Story. How appropriate that her friend had used that particular word because it had all been just that. A story.

"Well, like I said I worked in politics from the time I graduated until…well, I'm still working in politics! I love it. I know some people think it's corrupt and unjust. And of course, there is some of that just like in anything else. But I thrive on the excitement. I love meeting people, and I get up each day wondering what new adventure is just waiting for me to finish my coffee."

"Sounds boring to me," Paula said. "But I know it is something you enjoy. Tell us about Brent. When did you meet him? Was he your first love?"

Annette smiled now that she was on safer ground. "He wasn't my first love, but he is my last and forever love. I dated a little in college but didn't really have the time. Those grades were important to me, and I had to put a lot of work into keeping them up. Then when I went to work, I was busier than ever. I was meeting people constantly. But it wasn't until Senator Jensen's campaign that I met Brent. He was fresh out of law school and had already passed the bar. Jacob Jensen was a friend of Brent's Uncle Max. Brent believe in Jensen and thought that working on his campaign would be good experience. And it was. It seems that we were thrown together every day, each of us working in our own field of interest. I think we were attracted to each other immediately, but we were so busy that we didn't recognize or acknowledge it until after the election. He proposed to me on my 28th birthday, and we were married on Valentine's Day. Brent went to work in a law firm in Austin that represented several political figures. We campaigned for several of them. In the summer we learned I was pregnant. Our son Joshua Travis Thackeray was born two days before our first wedding anniversary. Then our daughter Judith Lydia was born two years and two months to the day afterwards. They are now nineteen and seventeen years old. Josh is attending Harvard and Lydia is a senior in high school."

"The end?" Karen asked.

"Pretty much."

"You left out a ton," Karen said.

Annette shrugged. "My life has been full of volunteer work. Scouts, Brownies, PTA, church, election campaigns. It's been a good life, a fun one. We met Wendell McMillan when he decided to run for governor, and Brent and I were both impressed from the very start. We campaigned and he is now nearing the end of his second term."

"And Brent is planning to run himself when the office is vacant," Paula said. "Is that what you really want, Annette?"

"It is," Annette said without hesitation. "I can do a lot as the First Lady of Texas. I can promote education reform. I want our criminal system revamped so that the punishment truly fits the crime. I'd love to see our health system become the best on the planet. And those are all Brent's goals too."

"Hey, no fair," Karen said. "We aren't supposed to strut our stuff until later."

They all laughed.

"I do apologize," Annette said. "And I'm sorry I'm so boring."

"That's what you get for being Miss Perfect," Karen said. "You've probably never done a shitty thing in your life."

How little you know, Annette thought. There were some things she would be happy now to let the others beat her in. But she seriously doubted they could in the Biggest Mistake of Life category.

Chapter 17

Karen Elizabeth Montgomery Douglas Payton Brewster

Karen Montgomery was the youngest of seven children and the only girl. Her brothers all insisted she was spoiled rotten, and she was. She liked it. But they had helped spoil her as much as anyone.

There were certain privileges to being the only girl. She didn't have to wear hand-me-downs that would be worn out before they reached her. She could cry if she wanted to though she seldom gave in to the luxury. It was worth biting the bullet or holding on until she was safely hidden in her room off the kitchen so that she didn't have to hear the taunting "crybaby" or "sissy britches." And she always got to choose Sunday night dessert.

But she didn't get excused from hard work. In some ways, she worked harder than her brothers. Karen would help her mother in the house. It wasn't easy keeping the place clean with seven males living there. Then she would carry two big baskets of food to the hay fields for her father's and brother's noon meal. After that, she stayed to help, sometimes by driving the tractor or driving the loaded truck back to the barn. By evening, she was as tired as everyone else and still had to help wash the supper dishes.

Bright and ambitious, Karen was the one who gave Annette the most competition in school. She was especially gifted in math, even helping Annette with tricky assignments once they reached high school. Karen was used to boys so was very comfortable around the opposite sex. She enjoyed flirting with them and particularly got a kick out of choosing boys she knew her brothers would not like.

Karen was the most athletic of the four friends. She and Annette played basketball and volleyball from the time they were first eligible in sixth grade until they graduated from high school. Stacy encouraged them by being a cheerleader most of that time. Only Paula didn't participate in sports though she usually attended the local games and cheered them on.

Graduation meant freedom to Karen, and she was ecstatic when she held the diploma in her hand. She worked the summer with her father. With her brothers now coming in only on weekends and during the summer, help was sporadic and unreliable. Claude Montgomery relied more and more on his daughter. When fall finally arrived, Karen took off in her six year old Volkswagen Beetle for Lubbock and Texas Tech. She lived with her brother Jerry and his wife Candace and their infant Marianna. That arrangement lasted her first year but was quickly not a situation Karen could endure any longer than that. Jerry Montgomery was as dominating and strict as their father. Too many weekends found Karen babysitting for her niece while her brother and sister-in-law were off golfing, attending a college game that Karen felt she should be watching, or taking a second (and third, ninth, hundredth) two-day honeymoon somewhere. Karen was reminded numerous times that this little service was fair exchange for free room and board.

By Christmas break of that first year, Karen knew that she couldn't stay at Tech though she liked the college. She transferred to the University of Texas at Austin and took two summer courses there while holding down a job at J.C. Penney's. Money was tight as she elected to rent a small on-campus apartment rather than move in with two other brothers, Mark and Eric. She had learned with Jerry that staying with her brothers was not a workable plan. Mark and Eric were both single, and Karen knew she would be doing all the cooking, cleaning, and laundry if it was to be done at all.

So she worked, studied, and partied every chance she got. During the summer between her sophomore and junior years, Karen had to move back home for lack of funds. Her father was getting older and had to sell part of the land to stay afloat. Karen helped all she could and worked part-time as a bookkeeper for a dress shop in Cullen. By fall, she was ready to go back to school but didn't have the means to do so.

Karen felt trapped. She couldn't stand the idea of living with her parents and settling for some minimum paying job that would not let her save enough to prepare for the future. So she took out a small loan and moved to San Angelo. She took two classes at the college there and worked full-time in a surveyor's office doing filing and typing. One day, a farmer and his son walked into the office.

Karen was not sure who noticed the other first. But Todd Douglas was one of the most attractive men she had ever seen even in his faded jeans, worn tee-shirt, and soiled baseball cap with "Booker's Feed and Seed" stitched in gold. She only knew that when their eyes met, there was something that she had never felt before. To her disappointment, Todd and his father quickly finished their business and was gone. They had done nothing more than exchange greetings and dozens of covert looks.

Sure that was the end of that, Karen was stunned the next day when she answered the phone with the usual "Baxter and Bruce, Surveyors" and heard a voice say, "Hey, pretty lady. This is Todd Douglas. Karen, right? I saw your name plate on the desk yesterday."

Karen was speechless for almost ten seconds. The she blurted out, "Hey, yourself. I hope you're calling to ask me out."

That was that. They were married over Christmas break. Karen's hope for a college degree in mathematics or business was dashed from that point. Instead, Todd's parents bought them a mobile home and set it up on the farm. Karen became responsible for even more work on her in-law's farm than she had on her own family's. Within two months she was pregnant with Donnie. A year after his birth, she had a second son, Randy. Karen's days became a round of feeding sheep, milking their one cow, diapers, cooking, cleaning, and endless laundry. By evening, she was so tired she could scarcely remember the dreams and goals she had once had. Then after three years of marriage, Todd suddenly started taking his own frustrations out on his wife by slapping her across the room or knocking her over the furniture. Then he drowned his guilt with a bottle of whiskey.

This physical abuse brought Karen out of her stupor. One day she packed up what few possessions she cared to keep, her sons and their clothes, and piled everyone and everything in her now ten year old car. She stopped in Bonnetville for her mother to see the boys. Her parents tried to talk her out of leaving Todd. But Karen's mind was made up. She didn't tell them how rough and abusive Todd had become. She just told them that marriage wasn't working out and it was best for her and the boys to leave while the boys were still young. When she realized there would be no help or support from her parents, Karen continued on down the road until she got to Austin. She had enjoyed attending college there and decided this was the place to stay. Her brothers no longer lived there, but Karen was determined that she and she alone would be responsible for herself and her two sons. She found a job as a clerk-typist in a small construction firm. She put her children in a reasonably priced day care not far from work and the small apartment she had rented.

And she enrolled in night classes at the university. One way or another, Karen was determined to get that degree.

"Okay, spill," Stacy said. She pulled the blanket tighter around her and looked in Karen's direction.

Paula had turned on the outside lights in her brother's house, but they didn't quite reach the cottage. She had also turned the lights on in the cottage, so there was a soft glow around them.

Karen took a deep breath. "Sadly, there really isn't that much to tell for thirty years. But here goes. After graduation, I had to stay and help on the farm. My dad was showing signs of slowing down, but the work still had to be done. Mom helped when she could, but she worked part-time as a bookkeeper for a couple of businesses in Cullen. Otherwise, there is no way they could have made ends meet. I remember thinking that I had been in such a hurry to grow up. And the first adult lesson I learned was that it sucked! I didn't see any of you anymore. Annette was gone a lot that summer. Stacy was working at the bank full time, and Paula was working and getting ready for her marriage to Gary. I think we only got together once that whole summer."

"That's right," Stacy said. "We had that slumber party the week before Paula's wedding."

"I almost backed out of marriage because of that slumber party," Paula said. Her voice was quiet. "I had so much fun, more fun than I had had in weeks, that I wondered if I really should be getting married."

"Guess you should have listened to your inner self," Karen said.

Paula shook her head. They couldn't see her, but they could

hear the smile in her voice.

"No, I don't regret it. It wasn't perfect, but there were a lot of good things. I have three wonderful children for one thing. Any of the bad was worth all of that. Go on, Karen."

"Well, that fall I went to Lubbock so I could attend Texas Tech. I made the mistake of living with my brother Jerry and his wife and baby. I think it would have been really good if I had stayed in the dorm that first year. Jerry was as bossy and nosy as my dad ever was. And because I wasn't paying any rent or for any food, they thought they could use me as an instant babysitter. I didn't mind doing it some of the time. Marianna was a sweetheart, and we're still close. But it didn't leave much time for me to have a social life. I decided not to stay at Tech though I really liked the school. So the summer after my year of college, I returned home to help on the farm. I should have gone and gotten a real, paying job. But I couldn't let my parents down. All of you had moved on, so it was really lonely and boring that summer. All I seemed to do was work, eat, and sleep."

"You mean there is more to life?" Paula asked.

They laughed, but it was weak. They suspected Paula wasn't kidding.

"Anyway, I decided to go to the University of Texas in Austin. I could have lived with a couple of my brothers there, but I had learned my lesson! I rented a small on-campus apartment and got a part-time job at Penney's. I really liked being on my own. I worked. I studied. And I partied every damn chance I got. That next summer, dad had to sell off part of the farm to stay afloat. My mom's health was beginning to fail. And the doctors couldn't figure out why. So I went home and helped dad. I also took over mom's bookkeeping jobs in Cullen. We thought if she had a break, it might help. My brothers got together and bought them tickets for Hawaii in August as an anniversary gift. I put in as much as I could, but I wasn't making a lot. When fall came around, I wanted to go back to school, but I didn't have the funds. And it was too late to apply for scholarships or to try and get a loan I knew I couldn't pay back. I had partied too much and then gotten stuck in this hick town."

"Oh, I don't know," Annette said. Ever the politician, she added, "It doesn't seem that bad now after having been to so many other places."

"Whatever," Karen said. "Anyway, I felt trapped. I definitely did not want to stay with my parents. So I took out a small personal loan and moved to San Angelo. I don't know why I picked San Angelo. I knew the college was there, of course. But I think someone had told me the cost of living was cheaper. And it was. I worked full-time in a surveyor's office doing filing and typing and go-fer stuff. I only could afford two night courses, but at least I was still working toward my goal of getting a degree in business or accounting or something with math."

"I thought you had a master's degree in accounting," Stacy said.

"I do now, but that was a long way down the road. Are you all going to keep interrupting me? We'll never get done."

"Go on!" the other three said together.

"Thank you. One day a farmer and his son walked in. That boy was the most beautiful fellow I had ever seen. He was fine. Dark brown eyes that crinkled at the corners when he smiled. And the smile! He was gorgeous. But he paid no attention to me! I was crushed. But the next day, he called me at the office and asked me out. We dated for three months, and I became Mrs. Todd Douglas over the Christmas break. That ended my schooling for awhile. I got pregnant right away and had Donnie less than a year after we were married. Then the year after that, I had Randy. I was working my butt off on his family's farm and trying to keep two boys under control. It was hard, and there was never enough money. Todd started drinking. And when he drank, he got mean. I got me and my sons out before he could hurt us."

"I should think so," Paula said. "Oh, sorry. Continue."

"I went to my parents. I guess I hoped they would have some suggestions. But they were horrified I had left Todd. They kept trying to talk me into going back. But I couldn't."

"Did they know he had become abusive?" Annette asked.

"Hell, no! I couldn't tell them that. I just said things had gotten bad, and it was better for me and the boys to leave. I don't know why I decided to go back to Austin, but that's where we ended up. I rented a small apartment and got a job as a receptionist and secretary. It was close to home and the day care center. Some days, I was able to take the boys to work with me. When the boss and men were out, they could play there. I was always glad for those days because it saved me a lot of money in child care. By that time, the boys were four and five. Donnie started kindergarten in the fall. I started taking a couple of night courses while the teenager next door babysat for me. Things continued like that for a couple of years. Todd never sent any money for the boys, and he never acted like he wanted to see them. He rolled his pickup one night after leaving a bar and was paralyzed from the waist down. I called him once, but he was so bitter. I couldn't expose the boys to that."

"You're telling us it didn't bother you at all when he was injured so badly?" Stacy couldn't imagine anyone that cold-hearted, and especially not one of her friends.

"Honey, I hadn't seen or heard from him in over three years. The one time I did call, he just wanted to know where the hell I had hidden his hunting knives. Not how are you or how are the boys. If it wasn't for the fact that Donnie looks so damn much like him, I'd have thought Todd was just a dream."

"So sad," Stacy said.

"Yeah. Anyway, I kept working at the same place and one day this guy walks in. He wanted to talk about adding a room to his house and making it handicapped accessible. He was a really nice guy, and I talked to him a lot while the boss was busy. His name was Ron Payton. His wife was seriously ill with lupus. It had come on suddenly and was advancing quickly. They had three kids only four, two, and eight months. We got to talking, and I offered to keep the kids if he ever needed me to. It turned out that he needed it soon and often. His wife developed thyroid cancer in addition to the lupus. She died seven months later before the room could even be built."

"How awful!"

"Stacy, if you keep--"

"Sorry, sorry. Go on."

"Well, Ron and I started doing some things together. Always with the kids. We took them to movies, ballgames, the park, on picnics, blah, blah, blah. After a couple of years, we realized that we got along really well. It just made sense for us to get married and make our family official. My boys were eight and seven. His oldest Justin was almost seven, Kara was five, and Martin was two and a half. It was great. We worked together well as a team. He was a teacher and I went to part-time work. We prepared meals together, did the laundry together. We just pitched in and did what had to be done. And as always, we involved the kids. We were married for five years."

"What happened? Whoops!" Stacy clapped a hand over her mouth.

Karen grinned. "Hard to keep quiet sometimes, isn't it? Roy wanted to go on a skiing trip to Colorado with some of his friends, some fellow teachers. It was something they had talked about for years. There were four of them. I encouraged him. I thought it would be fun for him to be with the guys for a change, and I thought he deserved the break. So when the school was off for a long weekend because of some holiday – President's Day or something – they decided to fly to Denver and rent a car to one of the ski resorts."

Karen's voice caught, but she quickly gained control. "On the morning they were to leave, I woke up hardly able to breathe. I was feeling a panic I've never known before. I don't remember dreaming. I just woke up almost hysterical. Ron tried to calm me. I clung to him and begged him to not go on the trip. I'll never forget the look on his face. I could see the disappointment, but I knew he would not go because I had asked him not to. We went back to sleep for a couple of hours before the alarm went off. He held me the entire time. When we got up, I told him he had to go on the trip. I apologized for being silly telling him I had some stupid dream about a monster trying to get in the house. He bought my story. He believed me!"

By now, Karen was crying. Stacy and Paula rushed to either side of her and Annette sat forward.

"They flew to Colorado as soon as school was out. He called that night after they reached the resort and again the next morning before they left to go skiing. He promised to call that night. I waited and waited. I knew something was wrong. I...I knew it. His friends finally called just before midnight. They had gone back to the resort around three to have a cup of coffee and warm up. Then they went out for one more run. They didn't miss Ron at first. They thought he had gotten back early and went up to take a nap. But when he didn't show for dinner, they got concerned.

They couldn't find him anywhere, and they alerted ski patrol. They finally found him at the base of a tree. He was still alive but died before they got him to the hospital. The doctors didn't think he would have survived even if they had found him right away. His skull was…he had no chance."

Karen's shoulders shook as she cried. Paula wondered if this was the first time she had really let go. They tried to comfort her, but some things can't be cured with a hug or soothing words. They let her cry, all three of them patting, stroking, and holding her. Finally, she took a deep breath.

"Water, please. Thank you. All right to finish this saga. I do want to say though that that marriage would have worked. It would have worked forever. But I had to go on with life. I now had five children to care for on my own. Fortunately, Ron had some insurance and his pension. But of course, it wouldn't be nearly enough to raise and educate five kids. I worked on getting my master's and I did it in a year and a half. There was a job fair at the college, and I met a very attractive, very charming man there representing the Houghton Accounting Agency in Houston. He gave me an application and then asked me to dinner. His name was Nicholas Brewster. He took my application back with him to Houston. In two weeks, I got a call to go for an interview. I got the job. Nick helped me find a house for me and my brood. We started to see a lot of each other. The kids liked him. Their ages were now thirteen down to almost eight. Nick proposed, but I wasn't sure he was ready to take on an immediate family, so I stalled him for another year and a half. But we got married. Later we had the twins, Tiffany and Mallory. We stayed married another four years and then divorced. There were some difference we couldn't seem to work out."

Differences that could have landed them both in jail and might yet.

"How old are the twins now?" Stacy asked.

Karen wiped her face with the palms of both hands. "Ten! Can't believe it. They aren't identical, but most people can't tell them apart until they know them well. One is very much into gymnastics and ballet. The other is an every other kind of sport's freak. They spend half of the time with me and half with Nick. The other kids are grown and out of the house now."

"So you still see Nick?" Annette asked.

"All the time. In some ways we are better friends now than when we were married. He's a good father. He's a good stepfather for that matter. But he just wasn't the man...I thought he was."

"Not the right man." Paula's words were whispered.

"I haven't met the right man," Karen said. "Yet."

Chapter 18

Paula Janine Lowe Clifton

"It's getting late," Paula said. "Maybe we should wait on mine."

"Nothing doing," Karen said. "We've talked. Now it's your turn."

"Well, at least, let's move inside. I turned the heat up, so it should be nice and toasty. I'll just put the chairs away."

Annette, Stacy, and Karen grabbed the blankets and glasses and cups and trooped in the small guest cottage. Paula folded the chairs and took them, two at a time, to the shed by the garage.

It wouldn't take long to tell her story, she thought. She had the least to share. Her life had been so routine, so boring. Well, maybe not exactly boring. But until the last few months, life had been predictable and...all right, boring. But it had been a comfortable existence until the divorce two years ago.

Like the others, she had gone to work after graduation. She had taken orders and payments in the very propane business her brother now owned. She hadn't really cared what she did so long as she earned enough money to buy the wedding dress she desired.

She had met Gary at a basketball game right after Christmas. He played for the opposing team. They had spotted each other across the court, and he had pushed through the crowds to meet her before their team bus left. At first their courtship had been limited to a few long-distance phone calls (on his part as her parents would never have allowed such an expense) and some letters. But when he turned eighteen in March, Gary had gotten a car. He started making the forty-five mile trip to see her on Saturdays. Before long, he was spending the weekends with her family, sharing a bed with William. Paula's parents liked Gary though they were concerned about them getting so serious. But Harold and Iona Lowe had married right out of high school, and that had worked out. So when Gary made a big production of asking both parents for Paula's hand in marriage, they were so charmed they consented. It hadn't mattered anyway. Both Paula and Gary were eighteen and didn't need parental consent.

Paula and Gary were married in August just before moving to North Texas State University where Gary had an athletic scholarship. Paula immediately found a job at the dean's office on campus. They settled down to college life. Gary practiced football for hours every day, coming home tired and grumpy. Paula spent the time alone reading and composing trivial poetry. She turned nineteen in November and became pregnant that night. Rebecca Suzanne was born the following July with no complications. Paula loved being a mother. She insisted that she couldn't continue working and still take care of the baby. Gary wanted to leave the child at the campus day care, but Paula insisted that she was the only one who could properly care for their daughter.

That resulted in their first big argument, but Paula prevailed. To compensate for the lack of income, she started babysitting and sold cosmetics door-to-door as her mother had done. They struggled through Gary's college career until he graduated with a degree in communications. By then Paula was pregnant with their second child.

Gary was hired to do the sportscast at a television station in San Antonio. Their son Troy Wayne was born there. After two years, Gary accepted a job in Galveston. Two years after that he was hired as news director and anchorman in Amarillo. When Becca was eight and Troy was six, they had Richard Harold who was named after both grandfathers. Paula's life became a series of birthday parties, playgroups, and business dinners. Gary thrived on being in the limelight. Still athletic, he played golf frequently and was on the city's men's softball team.

Paula took the children to church every week and taught them manners and how to be decent, honest citizens. Her family was her whole life, and she loved it. But something happened that shook her faith and rocked her marriage.

Eventually she regained her faith but the marriage was never stable again. The children grew up and suddenly Paula was left with nothing to do, no one to care for. Her parents died within months of each other, so she didn't even have that line to rely on any more. She tried her hand at writing short stories but had no success in having them accepted for publication. Volunteer work helped some. Gary liked her to do that because it made him look good. But Paula felt that life was passing her by, and she didn't know how to hop back on.

"Come on!" Karen called. "Stop stalling. We've told you what we've been up to. Come give us our lowdown."

Paula sighed and closed the shed door.

This wouldn't take long. She would be in a nice warm bed in just a few minutes.

They made themselves comfortable in the small cottage. Paula and Stacy stretched on the double bed, their backs propped up by the pillows. Annette sprawled in the one easy chair, and Karen sat on the floor and flexed her legs.

"My story starts out pretty much the same as all of yours. After graduation, I worked at the propane company taking orders and payments. And I planned my wedding to Gary. We got married the ninth of August. We spent our weekend honeymoon in Fort Worth going to the zoo and the botanical gardens. Then we settled in a little apartment in Denton. It was near the campus. After he graduated, we moved to San Antonio where Gary did the sports on one of the television stations. After a couple of years, he got bored and started looking for another position. He was hired by a station in Galveston. One hurricane and that was enough for him. So we were there for only a couple of years, too. That's when we moved to Amarillo, and that's where we stayed. I don't know why he likes Amarillo so much, but he's really made a place for himself."

"I liked Lubbock that year I was there," Karen said. "Except for the sandstorms."

"Amarillo is a hundred miles north of there. It gets cold. A lot colder than here. I always hated the cold, but Gary never minded. Anyway, we settled there. Gary started out as a reporter. Then he was an anchorman. And now he's the news director. He's good at what he does, but it's also the most important thing in his life. Never mind. When Becca was eight and Troy was six, we had Ricky. And Gary stated that was definitely, absolutely all the children he wanted. Despite my objections, he had a vasectomy."

"Real man," Karen said with an exaggerated drawl.

"Oh, come on, Karen," Annette said. "A lot of men have vasectomies. It doesn't meant they aren't real men anymore."

"Oh, has Brent had one? That could affect the way I vote." Karen ran a hand through her short spiky hair and grabbed her purse for a cigarette but remembered she had left them on the night stand back at the hotel.

"I didn't say that," Annette said, her voice edging on anger. "I just--"

"Yes, yes, yes," Karen interrupted. "I know they can still perform. It's more an attitude. They aren't man enough--"

"So," Paula practically shouted. "My life was centered on my family. I gave birthday parties, took groups of kids trick-or-treating, and drove carpools. I became the arm ornament for Gary at endless parties and benefits. I cooked, I baked, and I cleaned. Little Miss Suzy Homemaker, I was. Every year, we took two weeks in the summer go camping and fishing in New Mexico. You have no idea how much I hate camping. Once I got to go to China with a church group but it was only for a few days. And I went with my sister Jana Sue to Las Vegas because she won a free trip and her husband couldn't go."

Karen looked up suddenly and gave Paula a questioning look. Paula saw it and looked away.

"Then three years ago, I suspected Gary was having an affair. At first, I was devastated. Then I was angry. One night, I told him I was going to Dumas to spend the night with a friend. Of course, I lied. What I did was hide down the street to see what he would do. I didn't have to wait long, and I didn't have to do any major detective work. I saw him pull into our garage with a woman in the car with him."

Stacy gasped. "Oh, my gosh! I know what I did when that happened to me. I ran. What did you do?"

Paula swaggered as much as she could while still sitting on the bed. "I gave them plenty of time to…ah, settle in. Then I calmly walked into the house. There was no noise, so I went straight to the bedroom. I could hear them then. I pushed open the door, turned on the light, and grabbed Gary's belt that was on the floor with all their clothes."

"And?" Karen was alert, all signs of fatigue now gone.

"I went berserk. I'm embarrassed about it now, but it was

therapeutic in a way. I started swing that belt making contact every time I could. The hussy was screaming and dodging. Gary was trying to untangle himself from the sheets. I screamed for that little tramp to get away from my husband, to get out of my house. I chased her down the hall and out the front door. I wouldn't let her back in for her clothes."

"You go, girl!" Karen cheered. The other two applauded.

"I was sure Gary would be livid. But he had the decency to know he was licked. No pun intended. Anyway, I kicked him out. He grabbed all their clothes and left. There was never any question of reconciliation. I could never have gone to bed with him again. And I could never trust him. Because I didn't work, I had no money of my own. So in the end, Gary got the house and most everything in it. I got a ridiculously small settlement and my car. I found a little garage apartment and went to work doing whatever I could. The kids were out of the house. Becca had graduated college and was getting married. They both left for Harvard to work on a master's and now a doctorate in biology. Troy finished college and started training to be an airline pilot. Ricky graduated high school and started college. I was alone."

"Ever regret it?" Annette asked, her voice soft.

Paula was silent for a moment and then she shook her head. "No. Not the marriage and definitely not ending it. I wish I had been better prepared financially. Every woman should have some funds of her own."

"What kind of work did you find?" Stacy wanted to know.

"I work two days a week at the main library. They knew me because I had been going there and doing volunteer work for years. I work two days a week as an aide in a nursing home. And I am on call the fifth weekday as a secretary temp. I don't get called very often, so I really have to conserve. I started writing again. I had written some when Gary was in college and Becca was napping. Then two years ago, a month after the divorce was final, two of my children's books were accepted for publication. They've done pretty well."

"I heard they have done really well," Karen said. "I read reviews of both in the paper. I've even read the books though my kids are too old for them. They're sweet and cute and very touching."

Paula smiled. "Thank you. Fortunately, I learned to do a little drawing, so I was able to illustrate them, too. Helps with the profits," she said with a grin. "I made one very short book tour, and I've spent the time since working on a young adult novel. I don't know how it's going to do, but I keep trying."

"You'll do it," Annette said. "One thing you've always had is determination."

"So there's my story. Feel free to leave so I can go to bed."

"Spoken like a true hostess," Karen said getting up and groaning. "Jeez, this floor is hard! I've enjoyed the evening, ladies. I'll look forward to seeing you all tomorrow. Where shall we meet and when?"

"My room," Annette said also standing and stretching. "I'll

provide dinner this time. Shall we get together say…oh, two o'clock?"

"And the purpose of this meeting?" Paula asked. Her tone was casual, but there was a definite hint of anxiety.

Annette noticed. She smiled. "I think we should get to the business at hand. The reason we're having this get-together. Tomorrow we should all be ready to share our accomplishments. Are we ready?'

"As I'll ever be," Karen said.

"Ready," Stacy said.

Paula nodded, but she looked grim.

They bid each other good night and Paula led them to their car, shining a flashlight before them.

"Oh, by the way," she said as they prepared to get into Annette's car. "I'll be moving to the Leisure Inn tomorrow. I don't know the room number yet, but I'll be seeing you."

"Why?" Stacy asked. She didn't hide the fact that she was surprised by this news.

"Why what? Oh, the move? William's two older kids will be coming in this weekend, and they are both bringing two or three friends. They need the cottage because there certainly isn't enough room in the house for everyone."

"But, I thought William offered you the cottage for the whole week," Stacy said.

"It's okay," Paula said, her voice making it plain she didn't want to discuss it. "I'll enjoy staying in a hotel. It will be a treat for me. See you tomorrow."

Annette, Karen, and Stacy drove silently down the dark, quiet streets. They let Stacy out in front of her niece's house and bid her a good-night. As they pulled up in front of the Leisure Inn, Karen turned to Annette.

"She can't afford it."

"I know," Annette aid. "But what can we do? I'd offer to share my suite but she would still have to get another room this weekend when Brent and the kids arrive."

"She can stay with me," Karen said. "No one will be joining me this weekend. "I'll call her first thing in the morning."

"Good luck with that," Annette muttered and shut off the car's engine.

Chapter 19

Goodnight to a Long Day

Paula waved as the car lights disappeared down the dark street. She returned to the cottage, locked the door, and fell upon the bed. She wanted to talk to someone. Never mind that she had just spent hours talking with Annette, Stacy, and Karen. She longed to talk to someone close. Her daughter Becca was one of her best friends. But Becca and her husband lived in Boston, and it was very early in the morning there. Troy was probably flying across the Atlantic either on his way to or from Paris.

Ricky would no doubt still be up in his dorm. But she wouldn't embarrass him by making a midnight mommy call. He wasn't that much of a conversationalist anyway.

The person Paula really wanted to talk to was out of reach in Alaska. She let a sob escape and then angrily clenched her mouth together tightly.

She had no right to Jace Collins. He was too young for her, only thirty seven. He lived in a world far different from hers and any involvement with him was sure to affect his career.

Still he had become her very best friend in the last several months. She cared more about him than she had ever cared about Gary. And the special thing was, she knew he cared about her, too. But enough? And was it right? No, she owed it to him not to let him get too close. For his own good.

What she wouldn't give to hear his voice right now.

Stacy bid Karen and Annette goodnight and quietly slipped into her niece's house. Everyone was in bed, where they should be at this hour. She gently closed the door to her temporary room in the den and turned on the desk lamp. Without any hesitation despite the hour, she punched in the numbers to her home phone. Daniel answered on the second ring.

"Darling! I'm so sorry to wake. But I just couldn't bear not to hear your voice."

His warm chuckle gave her goose bumps and she wished she was in bed beside him.

"I wasn't asleep, love. I just turned the light out not two minutes ago."

She glanced at the clock. "But Daniel! It's midnight! Why are you up so late?"

"Just reviewing my last chapter. I'm excited to have you proof it for me, Stacy."

"I'm excited to read it!" Stacy kicked off her shoes and tucked her feet under her. "Daniel! Was that a cough?"

He cleared his throat. "Just a small one, dear. I may be coming down with a cold."

"Oh, Daniel! I should be home where I can take care of you."

"Nonsense! How is the visit going with the girls?"

"I want you to go to Dr. Barnes first thing in the morning. Do you hear me, Daniel? I don't want you getting sick. I want you here this weekend. I can hardly wait to see you."

He sighed. "All right, Stacy. If there is even a hint of a sniffle, I'll give him a call. Now about your visit."

"It's going well. It's really wonderful to see them all again. I can't believe it. We've all changed so much. And yet, we haven't changed at all. Do you know what I mean?"

"Of course. What plans do you have for the money?"

She gasped and then laughed. "Daniel Douglas Durfey, I know what you're doing! You're trying to distract me. It won't work. I'm calling you at noon tomorrow. I want a good report from Dr. Barnes. How is Austin?"

"Well. Missing his mother but too macho to admit it. He says I don't make pizza as good as you do. I thought all frozen pizza was the same, but apparently you have a knack I don't possess. What if you do get the money, Stacy? What will you do with it?"

"What would you have me do with it?" She knew the answer, but she wanted to keep him talking. She had never felt as homesick in her life as she felt at that moment.

"I think it would be a wonderful nest egg for your old age."

She closed her eyes to prevent the tears. Her old age, not "our" old age. Nothing ever upset her as much as thinking of a future without Daniel. May he live forever, she begged.

"I don't want to think about it now, Daniel. I just want you to promise me that you'll see Dr. Barnes first thing in the morning. You know how prone to bronchitis you are."

"Yes, dear." His tone was meek, but she would hear the grin. "I'll bid you a good night now. Why don't you wait until later to call tomorrow so you can catch Austin, too?"

"Noon. Then I'll call again in the evening. Good night, darling."

Annette had forgotten her cell phone on the dresser in her room and was not surprised to see that she had missed six calls, all from Brent. She never considered the time as they were often up late. She called as she undressed.

"'Bout time, wife!" His voice bellowed and she laughed.

"You old phony. Like you've been sitting there waiting for me to call." She dropped on the bed, totally naked. "What's so urgent?"

"In the first place," he drawled, "I have been sitting here waiting for you to call. True, I was also sleeping. But I was waiting. Second, what are you wearing?"

"Nothing."

He sighed. "I wish I could see that. Have you been gone only three days? Seems like weeks. Anyway, two things and then I'll let you catch some sleep. I have an eight o'clock meeting with the governor."

She stretched and flexed her feet. "What two things? And

what is the meeting about?"

"The meeting's about the Governor's Conference in Chicago next week. He wants me to go with him. You can tag along, too if you like." He was teasing. He seldom traveled without her if he could help it, and she knew it.

"The next thing is that Josh will be coming in this weekend. He says if this homecoming is important to you, it's important to him, too."

She bolted upright, squealing. "Brent! He's coming! I can hardly wait to see him. It seems like months instead of only…what? Seven weeks? But I can't imagine why in the world he would think this silly homecoming is anything important. As far as I'm concerned, the homecoming is nothing. It's meeting with the girls again that is so special. And I doubt he would find that very intriguing."

"I guess I should have told the news in a different order," Brent said. "Do you know a Tom Mackey?"

Annette frowned. "Tom Mackey? The name is familiar. Oh! I think he was a friend of my brother's. Tom Mackey? Yes, I'm sure he and Les hung out together. Why?"

"He called tonight and said that you have been chosen as Coming Home Queen. You'll be riding in a convertible around the football field at halftime and be Grand Honoree at the dance afterwards. Congratulations, your majesty!"

She was silent for so long Brent became worried.

"Annie?"

She shook her head. "I'm here. I'm just…I wish they hadn't done that. They haven't announced it or anything, have they?"

Brent was puzzled and didn't bother to hide it. "I believe they plan to tomorrow. Why? I thought you would be pleased. It's good publicity, honey. The home town girl and all."

Publicity. Of course, it was always about being in the limelight.

"I was thinking more of how this might affect the girls. I don't want there to be any hard feelings over something like this."

"Why should there be?"

Men could be so naïve. Or stupid. Maybe there wasn't a difference.

"Brent, I guess this is an honor. But it's one that any number of other women could just as easily--"

"But you're the one they picked. And it gets you in the public's eye. This will still be fresh when we announce my candidacy next month."

"I know, but--"

"We didn't ask for it, honey. This is a gift. My mother taught me that it is rude to refuse a gift."

She knew he wouldn't understand, and maybe it didn't matter. "Okay. Okay. I'm queen. Do me a favor and bring that navy blue suede pantsuit. I'll wear that instead of what I had planned. Everything else there okay?"

"Everything's fine. Lydia got an A on the English report. And she's wrangled money for a new outfit to wear this weekend."

Annette groaned. "Oh, lord, don't let her go shopping on her own. Get your speechwriter to take her. Sandy's young enough that Lydia will listen to her. And Sandy has enough fashion sense to keep Liddy in line. Got it?"

"Got it. You ladies decided yet who gets the money?"

"Not yet."

"What are you going to do with the money?"

"What? There's no guarantee that I'll get it, Brent. You're not counting on it, are you?"

"Of course not, sweetheart. But I can't imagine anyone else would be as deserving as you are."

"Well, they are. What would you do with the money?"

"Seriously?"

"Seriously."

"I think I'd go on a safari. I've always wanted to do that."

Annette ogled into space. "What? You would kill wild animals and mount their heads in our living room?"

He roared with laughter. "Hell, no! Too many of the voters would be after my head. They'd be happy to mount me on the state capitol! But it would be fun to go. Listen, I better get some rest so I don't fall asleep when the governor starts one of his long-winded stories. Sleep well. And listen, put some clothes on. Save all that natural beauty for me."

Karen's phone was ringing as she unlocked the door to her room. It startled her. Who in the world would be calling at this hour? She snatched up the phone and demanded, "What?"

"Hi, Mom! It's me, Tiffany."

She let her breath out and sat on the edge of the bed. "Tiffany Amber Brewster, what in the world are you doing up at this hour?"

Her daughter's voice became very prim and proper. "What in the world are you doing out this late, Mother? We've been trying to call you all evening. Do you have your cell phone turned off again?"

"Who is we?"

"Me and Mallory, of course. We want to know when you're coming home."

Karen ran a hand through her hair, leaving it even spikier. "What difference does it make? You're with your father this week anyway."

"We know, but we miss you. And we don't have to go to school tomorrow!"

"Why not?"

"Water break. Or something like that. Can you be home by Sunday? I have a gymnastic meet then."

Karen could see her daughter sprawled on her stomach on the bed, feet kicking air. "I don't know what time I'll be in Sunday. I'll try to make it, but I can't promise."

"Okay-doke. I hope you can though. Mal wants to talk to you."

"Hi, Mommy. Isn't it great we don't have school tomorrow? Even Daddy's glad because he said he'll just have to take off work to babysit us. Isn't that cute? Like we need a babysitter. Are you going to get the money, Mom? Cause I really need some hockey equipment. This old stuff I got is junk?"

"I don't know who will get the money, Mallory. But for now, I want you and Tiffany to go to bed. Give each other a kiss for me and I'll see you in a few days."

"I love you, Mommy. Talk to you soon. Bye!"

"Good-bye. And good night," she added firmly.

Karen propped herself against the bed and thought about her daughters. She did miss them. But it was also nice to be away for awhile. They were very energetic, demanding girls who often robbed her of any self-time. Before Karen could ponder her motherhood, the phone rang again. Frowning, she grabbed it.

"It told you to go to bed!"

Obviously, the caller was not one of the girls.

"Hello?"

"I was just wondering if you were serious," the voice said. "I don't remember you telling me to go to bed. But if that's an invitation--"

"It's not! I mean, I thought you were one of my kids calling again. Anyway, what are you doing calling this late?"

"It's no longer late," Ryan said. "In fact, it is now officially early. And if you had been in sooner, I would have called earlier. How is the Fearless Foursome getting along anyway?"

"Fine. You'll probably see us all at the Pancake Supper."

"Not until then, huh? I thought I had an invitation--"

"Go to bed, Ryan. You own bed! Good night."

And so ended the day for four women who wished they were in other places with other people safely distanced from the point they thought they had outgrown.

Chapter 20

Preparing for Stage One

Paula spent Tuesday morning cleaning the little cottage, changing the sheets on the bed and doing her laundry. Claire invited her to lunch and Paula enjoyed the chicken over rice and stir fry vegetables when William came in at noon. They laughed and reminisced as they ate.

As he prepared to return to work, William said to his wife, "Did you ask her yet?"

"No," Claire said, playing coy.

"Ask me what?" Paula asked as she stacked dirty dishes.

"Go on," William prompted.

Claire made a silly face and pretended to take a deep breath. "I'm going to Hazelwood tomorrow for a hair appointment. I wondered if you would like to go and have Chinese afterwards. Real Chinese. Not the stir fry we had today. My treat. I didn't know your plans with the girls, but I was hoping maybe…if you'd like."

Paula immediately tried to think of a good reason to decline and then realized there really was no reason to do so. She smiled at her sister-inn-law.

"I don't think we have any special plans early. We've been trying to include family in our days, too. Sure, I think that would be fun. I love Chinese."

Claire beamed. "Great!"

William nodded at her and Claire spoke again. "I don't know how to say this. I don't want you to take it the wrong way. But...well, we've missed some of your birthdays."

Some of her birthday! Paula couldn't remember one time they had remembered her birthday.

"I've tried to miss a few of them myself," she said hoping her joke would encourage Claire to get on with it.

"Well, I was just thinking. It's such a treat to get your hair done, isn't it? I love that. And I was wondering if you would like to...you know. Have something done. A trim? Touch-up. Something. Not that there is anything wrong with your hair now, Paula! I didn't want to say anything because I didn't want you to get the wrong idea. But...well, William and I would like to treat you with a hair appointment if you will let us. Kind of like a late birthday present."

"Or an early one," William said. "You do have a birthday coming up, sis. But you're never around then. We were trying to think of something special, and Claire suggested this. She always acts like she's been to the moon or something after getting her hair done."

Paula almost laughed out loud. She knew they were trying to

make up for wanting her out of the cottage. Well, why not! It was all working out okay anyway. She had the hotel room, and she would enjoy that just as much as the cottage.

She nodded. "Sure. That sounds great! I could use a trim. What time? So I can let the girls know my schedule."

Claire clapped her hands and smiled. "I'll call Renee and tell her we want the ten o'clock appointment. My appointment is at eleven. Then we can eat. I have to get back for a PTA meeting at three. We have to finalize the plans for Homecoming Weekend. So can you be ready to leave at nine? I'll pick you up."

"I'll be ready."

Karen was waiting in the parking lot when Stacy pulled in.

"Thought I better meet you. We decided to hold our gathering today in Paula's room. You wouldn't know where to go since we thought we would be in Annette's room."

"That's fine," Stacy said. Her smile was bright and her step light. She had talked to Daniel who had dutifully gone to the doctor. The doctor said her husband was fine but gave him some medicine to ward off any approaching illness. She was so relieved, she practically skipped into the hotel.

"I think it's too bad Paula had to move out of that cute little cottage," Stacy said as she linked arms with Karen. "I know she can't afford this."

"Woo-hoo!" Karen said. "Wait until you see her room. Annette is practically drooling. It makes our rooms look like slumming."

Stacy frowned. "What? But how can that be?"

Karen shrugged as she stepped into the elevator. "This mystery friend of Paula's. Evidently, he reserved the room. What am I saying? It's not a room! It's a suite! It has a refrigerator, a microwave, a huge TV set. Even Paula was stunned when she saw it. But she recovered fast I must say. Know what she said?" Karen mimicked Paula. "She said, 'This is a little more than I need.' No kidding!"

Paula opened the door almost before they finished knocking. Stacy did her best to not be surprised, but the room was enormous and much more elaborate than the others. The four had barely settled themselves when another knock interrupted them.

Paula answered the door and took a huge bouquet from a maid. It was an assortment of colored roses, white lilies, daffodils, and baby's breath in an amber cut glass vase.

"Wow!" Karen could not resist saying.

Paula blushed. She set the flowers on the table, took the card out of the envelope, blushed even redder, and slipped the card into her purse.

"Well," she said. "How did everyone spend their morning? I cleaned the cottage and then lunched with William and Claire. Oh, and before I forget, I'm going with Claire tomorrow to Hazelwood, but we'll be back by early afternoon."

"I slept in," Annette said.

"So did I," Karen said. "Then I went to visit Daddy."

"How is he?" Paula asked. She was being polite while still trying to overcome being so flustered. "Did he know you today?"

"No," Karen said. "I doubt he'll ever know me. But I know him."

"I just visited with my niece and then called Daniel."

"So now we're all ready to get down to business, right?" Annette said.

Paula stood suddenly and started for the bedroom. "Hold on until I go to the bathroom. There's ice and soft drinks in the refrigerator. Help yourselves."

The three watched her leave.

"Methinks the lady needs a moment to compose herself," Annette said drily.

"Should we look at that card?" Karen asked, looking pointedly at Paula's purse sitting on the table by the door.

"No!" Stacy hissed when it appeared that Annette was considering Karen's question. "We can't do that! She'll tell us when she want us to know."

"What if she doesn't want us to know?" Karen said. "I want to know. Don't you want to know? Who laid out the money for this set-up? I mean honestly. A three bedroom suite. And who sent that whole floral shop? I just want to know what his name is. And if he has a brother! What's one little peek going to hurt?"

"No!"

Paula returned carrying four sheet of hotel stationary and pencils. She passed them around and flopped into a chair.

"We probably should take notes, don't you think?"

"That must be the writer in you," Karen muttered. "What kind of notes?"

Paula looked offended and then embarrassed.

"I just thought--"

Annette scooted in closer to the table and put her paper on it. "Notes are a great idea. Today we'll pat ourselves on the back. Tomorrow we'll repent of our sins. And Thursday, we'll state our goals for the future. Ready, set...who goes first?"

Chapter 21

Lauds and Applauds

Part One – Annette's Accomplishments

"Let's go alphabetically," Paula said.

"First names or last?" Karen asked.

"First."

They looked at Annette who wrote "My Accomplishments" on the top of her paper.

"Well," she said. "Well, well, well. Where to start. Humm. Really, I've been thinking about this for several months, and the things I'm most proud of are things that aren't so impressive to others."

"Quite stalling," Karen said.

"Okay! Now this is just since high school, right?"

"Annette!" Karen sat up and leaned toward her friend. "What's wrong with you? You've known this was coming, so why are you suddenly so shy about tooting your own horn. What horn did you play anyway? It was a flute, wasn't it? Did you ever do anything with that?"

Annette laughed, enjoying Karen's impatience. "No. Of

course not. I don't think I've even touched the thing since high school. I'm not even sure where it is now. Okay. Here we go. I graduated from A&M with honors."

"Impressive," Stacy said. "That's not an easy school."

"School," Karen said. "Does school count?"

"Yes!" Stacy and Paula said together.

Karen shrugged. "Okay, go on."

"I was elected mayor of Sullivan when I was thirty. That's right out of Austin. Just a small town. I served only one term because I started having my children. I've served on various boards and committees mostly having to do with education reform and health care. I've helped on several election campaigns with my candidate getting elected. I'm hoping our luck holds when Brent runs!"

"It's too bad he hasn't already run," Paula said. "Then you could count being First Lady of Texas."

Annette smiled. She did love the sound of that.

"I organized and directed a relief operation seven years ago when that monster tornado hit Taylor County. And I guess my favorite accomplishment is helping to establish and stock libraries in twenty-four small towns across the state. I did that twelve years ago, and all but one of them is still functioning and growing."

"What happened to the other one?" Paula asked.

Annette shrugged. "Fire. Probably arson. We didn't bother to start it up again because there didn't seem to be the interest."

"Especially if they were going to burn it down again," Paula pointed out. "Too bad. Libraries are a vital service to a community. I work in one twice a week. Did I tell you that?"

Karen sniffed and switched her gaze from Paula to Annette.

"Anything else?"

Annette made a wry face. "I have a marvelous husband and two terrific kids. I don't know if you want to consider that an accomplishment, but I sure do. Even if it is just a personal one."

"Fine by me," Karen said. "Do you want to name all those boards and committees?"

Annette pulled papers from her briefcase, removed a paper clip and handed the stapled sheets to each of the others. There were a page and a half of listings. Committees, boards, charities, all neatly typed, single-spaced.

"You get the picture. I'm civic minded."

"That's an understatement," Paula said. She sneaked a look at Stacy and Karen and was relieved to see them look as concerned as she did. Would any of them be able to top Annette's accomplishments?

"I don't know why you're bothering to encourage Brent to run for governor," Karen said as she skimmed the pages. "Why don't you just throw your hat in the ring?"

Annette smiled. "I thought I'd let him break in the job for me."

"Are you serious?" Stacy asked with a squeal. "You really think you would run?"

"No way!" Annette answered. Her laugh now reflected

amusement. "I'm very happy being behind the scenes. You won't catch me pulling a Hillary Clinton."

"Make a note of that," Karen said. "We'll see what happens in a few years."

"You won't be behind the scenes on the campaign trail," Paula reminded her. "You'll be right up front for everyone to see."

For the briefest of moments, an expression passed over Annette's face that looked very much like dread or even fear. But apparently only Paula noticed.

"Annette?"

Annette recovered quickly. "That's okay because I'll be doing it for Brent. Really, I think that covers my accomplishments. It sounds pitifully lacking considering I seem to stay so busy all the time."

"It if sounds pitifully lacking," Karen said. "it's because you don't care to elaborate. If you were to describe the work of all these committees and boards and things...but I think we get the picture. Thanks for sharing. You're always free to add to the list if you think of something else. I'll save room on my sheet. I guess I'm next. Mark your sheet. Karen's Great Contributions and Accomplishments to the World. Here I go."

Part Two – Karen's Accomplishments

"Three husbands and seven children."

Everyone grinned but no one wrote anything down.

"Well, one of those husbands was an accomplishment," she

said stubbornly. And the kids are all pretty great."

"Good start," Stacy said. "What else?"

Karen growled. "This is going to be a tough audience. I got a master's degree in accounting. Okay? Will that one work?"

Annette, Paula, and Stacy made exaggerated marks on their papers.

"And I...well, I don't know if this counts. I sing."

"You sing?" Paula echoed.

"Yes, sing. Ahh, ahh, ahh, ahh."

"Like in the shower?"

"No smarty pants. Like in public. I sang in the church choir for several years. Yes, I have been known to go to church more than twice a year. And I sang the national anthem at a gymnastics meet last year. I've sang at several weddings and funerals."

"Seriously?" Annette asked. "Are you any good?"

"Of course, she's good," Stacy said. "Don't you remember she was in the glee club? She sang that special one Christmas."

"I'm good enough that I don't embarrass myself," Karen said with no attempt at modesty.

"Great!" Annette said. "You can sing at Brent's inauguration."

"That's good," Paula said. "What else?"

Karen took a deep breath. "On a more serious note, I managed to save a senior citizen housing center from being demolished. I brought the newspaper clipping," she said as she pulled a clipping from a folder. "It was eight years ago. Some rich business tycoon guy wanted the land for a parking lot. It was going to displace several dozen elderly people. Made me so damn mad. So I took on the guy. I stirred up the public and we managed to pay the back taxes and they still have their homes."

"Karen, this is really good," Stacy said as she read the clipping with Annette and Paula. "This is the kind of stuff we were talking about thirty years ago. Not that your achievements aren't good, too, Annette. They are. I'm proud of both of you."

"This is excellent," Annette said and handed the newspaper article back to Karen. "And knowing you, I'm sure this isn't all."

Karen shrugged. "I did do one other thing that I think is worth mentioning. I also helped keep a small hospital going. It was in Muller, which is a very small town. It's close to where one of my brothers lives in West Texas. This hospital was their only medical facility for almost a hundred miles. My brother asked if I would look into it. Since I'm good with numbers, I managed to help them pay off some bills and bring in more money without burdening the patients. I also showed them how they could better manage what resources they already had. It was hard because I don't know that much about medicine. But I do know numbers. Ahem," she said holding up another newspaper clipping. "This was around twelve years ago."

Paula chewed her bottom lip as she read this article and then passed it to Annette who shared with Stacy.

"Math always was your thing," Paula said. Her voice was strangely strained. "I do well to balance my checkbook. And I

FRIENDS*ENEMIES

don't have that much to balance."

"Congratulations, Karen," Annette said. "You have done a couple of wonderful things. What else?"

Karen shrugged. "Not much. I'm only good for one major thing a decade, and I haven't done this decade's yet."

"Come on," Stacy urged. "Don't be so modest. I know you've done other things."

"Honestly, not that much." Karen reached for her drink. "Raising the kids kept me pretty busy especially when I was a single mom. Oh, well, I did serve as PTA president a couple of times. I was a Boy Scout leader. I've driven a lot of carpools. I've served on a few committees but nothing big or that demanding. No, I guess I gave you the gist of it. Your turn, Paula."

Paula smiled though it was weak. "Didn't you tell me once...oh, many years ago. I think you were still married to your first husband. Didn't you rescue an old woman from her burning house?"

Karen's mouth dropped open. "I'll be damn! I forgot all about that! I did save her. And got my ass chewed out by every fireman who responded. But if I had waited until they got there, the smoke would have got her. Men are such idiots."

Paula grabbed her drink. "I'll drink to that."

Annette and Stacy both shook their heads. "Can't drink to that," Annette said. "I think my man has some brains."

"Me, too," Stacy said with a smile.

Karen and Paula looked at each other, touched their cups

151

together and then drank.

"Well, I think that wraps it up for me," Karen said wiping her mouth with the back of her hand. I'll let you know if any more heroic adventures resurface from my subconscious. It's your turn, Paula," she said firmly. "I know you're trying to get out of doing this. And lady, it ain't a-going to work."

Part Three – Paula's Accomplishments

Paula wasn't sure why she was there. Obviously, her achievements couldn't begin to stack up against those of Annette and Karen. Suddenly her entire life seemed wasted. And because her marriage failed, she felt like a failure, too. She tried to think back to those days when she had had high ambitions and a drive to succeed at whatever she tried. She couldn't remember them.

The other three watched her, pencils posed. She offered a weak smile.

"I'm afraid I haven't done anywhere nearly as much as you two. I do have great kids. Really they are. Becca's working on her doctorate in biology. Troy is employed as an airline pilot. Ricky's still in school, but I know he'll be okay once he settles down and decides what he wants to do."

"Good kids," Karen said and wrote that on her paper.

The three of them watched her again. She wanted to cry but knew how inappropriate that would be. Oh, why had she even bothered to come? Or why hadn't she thought more about this stupid pact and worked on making a decent showing. She sighed.

"There's really not much, I'm sad to say. I mean, I've lived a pretty good life. I've done the normal things like being room mother and serving on the PTA and church boards. I did the choir a favor by not joining them," she said in an attempt to lighten things. The others smiled. "I did serve on the National Read Now committee, and we were successful in getting more people of all ages to read. It was great. I helped with the cleanup and disaster relief when Amarillo had the big tornado six years ago. So I understand how much effort you put in on the relief in Taylor County after their tornado," she said to Annette. "I also helped set up a donation center when the grass fires spread across the state last year." She brightened a bit. "I have written two children's books that are a bit successful. One even got an award. I'm working on a young adult novel at the moment and do have a publisher who is willing to look at it."

"Great!" Stacy said. "What's it about?"

Paula shook her head. "Can't tell you. Sorry, but it's bad luck to talk about it before the first draft is done. Jinxes thing somehow."

"I understand," Stacy said. "Daniel never allows me to read his work until all his thoughts are on paper. Those are great achievements, Paula. What else?"

Paula shook her head. "That's about it really."

Karen gave her an inquisitive look. But before she could speak, Annette said, "Wait a minute. I know that's not all. I remember hearing about an incident when you lived in Galveston.

It was on the news even in Austin, and my cousin sent me a newspaper article from Beaumont. You do know what I am talking about, don't you?"

Paula blushed and shuffled her papers though they were already in a neat pile. "That was nothing," she said. "I really don't want to talk about it."

"What?" Karen and Stacy asked together.

"Go on, tell us about it," Annette urged. "I remember thinking at the time there goes our fund."

"Tell us!" Karen said.

Paula shrugged and made little circles on her sheet of accomplishments. "I don't think it is any more special than you rescuing the woman from a burning house. But there was this…situation. I had gone to the bank, and a man there pulled a gun."

The shocked gasp came from Stacy.

"He didn't…he wasn't trying to rob the bank. He just wanted to use the bank building. He made five of us go to the roof with him. Then he had us sit down against the edge of the roof. Our backs were against the little part that rose up. Anyway, he was very distraught. His wife had left him. His child had a brain tumor. He lost his job. He couldn't find help anywhere. He couldn't see any way out and decided that he might as well take a few others with him. He had a high powered rifle. I don't know anything about guns, but it was mean looking. He shot off some rounds at the people on the street. He never hit anybody, and he never hurt any of us hostages. I don't think he really wanted to do anything bad. He was in so much despair, he honestly didn't know what he was doing. At least, that's how I felt at the time."

"What happened?" Karen asked.

Paula frowned. "Well, after three hours of sitting out in the hot sun and worrying about my children who were with the next door neighbor I started trying to talk to him. The cops had the streets blocked off, and they kept trying to get to the roof but the door was locked and he had pushed some stuff in front of it. They tried to send a helicopter over, but he shot at it. I think he would have shot it down if he could have. For some reason, seeing the helicopter made him mad. But to make a very long story – about nine and a half hours long – much shorter, I finally talked him out of shooting anyone on the ground or any hostages. I convinced him there was help, and I would make an effort to see that he got it. Finally, he let the police in. They took him to jail, and we all went home. That was it. End of story. Unpleasant at the time but hardly a major achievement."

There was silence for a good minute. Then Annette said, "I would call that a very significant achievement. What happened to the guy?"

"He went through a lot of psychological testing. People testified that he had always been a great guy, very kind and generous. He just snapped. He was sent to a mental hospital for about three years. Then he was released. I kept in touch with him even after we moved to Amarillo. He always said," she stopped talking and reddened with embarrassment. "Well, that's it."

"He always said what?" Stacy wanted to know.

Paula found it hard to continue. She smiled and looked away. "Oh, it was silly. He just said I was his guardian angel. That's so funny. There's nothing angelic about me."

"There are avenging angels as well," Karen pointed out.

"Thanks a lot!"

"I just mean, you probably were some type of angel to him. You helped him when he needed it. And that's more than a lot of people can say. How could you forget to mention this? Or why would you not think this was important. Whatever happened to him?"

Paula bowed her head but not before they saw the tear ooze out one eye and slide down her cheek. "Wouldn't you know it? He got things together. Then he was killed in an oil rig accident in the Gulf of Mexico."

"Poor man," Stacy said.

Paula nodded. "It seemed like such a waste. Another one of my failures."

"What?" Annette stopped writing and looked at Paula. "Failure? This is not a failure. You have no control over other people's lives. Just because it didn't turn out the way we all think it should have doesn't mean it was a failure."

"Whatever," Paula said, her voice scarcely audible.

Karen snorted, and that shook Paula from her dreamy state.

"That's my story. I guess we're ready for you now, Stacy.

This is going quick, isn't it?"

"Wait a minute," Karen said. "Paula, you haven't even mentioned one of your greatest accomplishments."

Paula's expression went blank. She shook her head. "I don't know--"

"Lilea."

"No!" The word came out in a strangled gust of air. "No, Karen."

"Why not? Paula, that was a wonderful thing."

"I will not use her for money."

"It's not using her. She's one of your--"

"I said no!"

The silence was so thick everyone shifted uncomfortably.

"I'm lost," Annette said. "Who is Lilea?"

No one spoke but all eyes were on Paula.

"Paula?" Stacy put a hand on her friend's arm. Paula shrugged her off.

"No."

"Oh, hell," Karen said. "All right, don't count her as an accomplishment. But don't you think you should at least mention her?"

Paula looked at Karen with pain that obviously ran so deep, she couldn't speak.

"Why did you have to say anything?" she asked. "Why couldn't you just keep your mouth shut?"

Karen recoiled as though Paula had slapped her. Then she

stiffened her lip and sat forward. "They have a right to know anyway. So I'll tell them. If you don't like it, take your gorgeous flowers and go to the other room."

Paula flinched this time. She reached for her water and drank deeply.

"This is what I know," Karen said to Annette and Stacy. "Remember that church trip to China Paula mentioned? Well, I don't know all the circumstances but Paula was able to adopt a Chinese baby. I remember it was unusual that they allowed anyone to do that. At least so quickly. But she did. She brought the child home, and raised her just like she did her other three children. Lilea was quite a bit younger. But if you know anything at all about China, then you know how horrible they were to baby girls back then. They would kill them by injecting poison or something in their brains. They would throw them in the Yangtze River. They got rid of them like they were unwanted kittens. Paula gave this child a chance in life. Sadly, the life didn't last as long as anyone would have liked. But Paula gave her quality existence. She would never had had that in China."

"Oh, my gosh," Stacy said. "I do remember getting a Christmas card once. I just assumed she was a foster child. What happened?"

Paula stared at the space between the dresser and window. "She died," she said in a whisper. "She had just turned eight and had been invited to a birthday party. I didn't want her to go. But she was so happy and excited. They were to go roller skating and then to a movie. The van they were in was broadsided by a truck. Lilea died on impact. The birthday girl was injured and took months to recuperate and rehabilitate. The other four girls and the mother only had minor injuries."

Stacy sobbed quietly and Annette sat with her hand over her mouth. Her eyes were bright with restrained tears.

"I loved her so much. But Gary…he never really accepted her. I guess I shouldn't have brought her home without him getting used to the idea first. But it was such a unique opportunity, and I was so sure he would come to love her. Then she died. She was a beautiful, wonderful special blessing in our lives. And that's why I will not use her. She was worth more than the fund could ever be."

"Of course," Stacy whispered. "All right, we understand. We do, don't we, girls? But it was a special and loving thing you did. I wish I had thought to do something like that. It never occurred to me to try and adopt. Thank you for telling us about her."

Paula nodded. But she continued to stare at nothing, tears coursing down her face.

"I call a break," Annette said. "We definitely need a break. I think I'll take a walk around the parking lot. Then Stacy we'll be ready for you."

"I'll go with you," Karen said and stood quickly.

"I'll stay with Paula," Stacy said and put an arm around her friend. She touched her head to her friend's forehead. "Just give us a few minutes."

"I'd never take that money if I thought I had to give up a child," Paula said.

"Of course not. The money isn't the important thing."

"I don't know if I even want the money anyway," Paula sniffed. "I really don't."

"It's okay. Don't even think about it. Sshh! Everything is going to be okay. Sshh!"

Part Four – Stacy's Accomplishments

When Annette and Karen returned to the room almost half an hour later, Stacy and Paula were laughing at something on their laps.

"Look," Paula said. "Stacy brought a photo album! I don't even know what happened to all the pictures and stuff I had from school. Look!" She squealed and pointed and then burst into laughter. "Karen, this was your western period."

A very young and extremely skinny Karen poised wearing jeans, a western shirt, a cowboy hat and cowboy boots. She stood with legs bowed, hat pushed back, and a piece of hay sticking out of her mouth.

Karen gurgled and lunged for the album, but Stacy grabbed it safely out of reach.

"No, you don't," she warned. "This is very special private property. But if you want to get even," she looked up and grinned evilly. Then she turned the photo album toward Karen who guffawed.

"Let me see that," Paula said and hung over Stacy's back. "EEEEEKKKK! Have you ever operated as a blackmailer these last thirty years?"

Stacy was laughing so hard she could hardly answer. "Oh, come on. This is adorable." Paula and Annette stood together wearing identical tent dresses, a fad in their senior year. The dresses flowed with no shape or style and made every wearer look pregnant. Not only were the dresses hideous in design, but Annette's was lime green and Paula's was brilliant orange.

"Let's see some picture of you," Annette suggested.

Stacy slammed the book shut and slipped it under her leg.

"Whoops! Would you look at the time! If we are going to the Firemen's Pancake Supper tonight, we better finish up here."

"Oh, that's right," Annette said. "I was going to treat us to dinner, but I suppose we better not turn down pancakes."

"We'll give you the privilege of treating us tomorrow night," Karen promised.

With boos and jabs and more laughter, the four women settled themselves down in the chairs around the table.

"First, I want to say that I am very impressed with each of you. What you have done with your lives is nothing short of inspiring." Stacy gave them each a look of love and encouragement. "I'm so proud to be part of this group. Thank you for your efforts and especially for your successes."

"Wait a minute," Karen said. "Does she get extra points for eloquence? I didn't make a speech, but I can."

"Not now, dear," Annette said and patted Karen's hand. "Stacy's right. We'll have to hurry to make that pancake supper. I agree with you, Stace. We've done well. And you'll probably put us all to shame. So lay it on us, lady."

Stacy smiled, took a deep breath, and started.

"I think I know how Paula feels. I mean about not feeling that she has done very much. But we have. They might not always have been huge things, but it's the little every day bits that really keep the world turning. I have been teaching school since I graduated from college. I've done mostly kindergarten and first grade. But I did teach junior high English for two years."

Karen said, "She's earned the money right there."

"Oh, hush! They're not so bad. It's a hard age for kids. They're trying to grow up but aren't quite there. One day their emotions are quite adult; the next they are like little kids again. Anyway, I've taught kids. So I've had the opportunity to touch a lot of lives. I hope it's been for the best. For the most part, I think it has. Of course, there are always those you don't know about."

"Can't save the whole world, Stace," Annette said.

Stacy nodded with a grim smile. "So true. Well, what else? I've served on the Accountability Committee at school for a number of years. I organized a tutoring program for the elementary school. We've recruited parents, civic leaders, and older students, anyone who could give kids a little one-on-one time. It's been remarkably successful. Our state assessment scores are up by thirty-six percent, and our students are showing a better attitude about learning. Also there have been fewer behavioral problems."

"You are definitely to be commended," Paula said. "My Troy had such a hard time with English, especially grammar. We could never get the teacher to understand that he was trying. She would never change her teaching style to help him."

"Sad to say, that happens all too often," Stacy said. "But not at my school," she added with a grin.

"What else?" Karen asked.

"I've taught Sunday school for the past twelve years. All different ages. They seem to move me around a lot, so I don't know if that is good or if they are giving the classes a break from me!"

They laughed and Annette poured everyone some water.

"Really, there's only one other thing that I can think would count."

"You have a great husband and wonderful son," Karen said.

"It's true, I do. But that's not what I'm talking about. That goes without saying."

"So?" Paula said. "What other thing?"

"Well, a few years ago, my fourteen year old nephew Perry got so sick and suffered kidney failure. I was able to donate one of my kidneys to him."

There was such a still silence that everyone seemed afraid to move.

"You're kidding," Paula said. "But that's wonderful! To give of yourself like that? Can there be anything more giving, more loving?"

"Yes." Stacy nodded her head emphatically. "Saving a woman from a burning building rates up there. Talking a sniper out of slaughtering innocent people is big on the list. Helping with education and health reforms for an entire state…that's big."

"How is your nephew today?" Annette wanted to know.

Stacy smiled. "He's a big strapping healthy deputy sheriff in Tarrant County. And he visits or calls his Aunt Stacy four or five times a week. We're very close."

"Wow." Paula looked at the others for comment as hers seemed to fit in the one word.

"Incredible," Karen said.

"Truly magnificent," Annette said.

Stacy blushed and stood. "Truly, that's it. My life is very much wrapped up in Daniel and Austin. I like it that way. I'm happy to help others as long as it doesn't interfere with my family. If there is nothing more, I need to get back to Nina's. I promised to go the Pancake Supper as their guest. And I want to call home. I haven't talked to Austin since I left."

"We all better get moving," Annette said also standing. "I have to meet my brother and his wife. What time shall we get together tomorrow?"

"I can't until afternoon," Paula said. "Like I told you earlier, I promised Claire I would go with her to Hazelwood."

"Okay," Karen said. "Let's make it something like two, okay?

My room this time. So we're going to bare our souls, aren't we? That should be fun."

"We don't need to elaborate on every little nitty gritty sin," Annette said. "We don't really have to tell anything we don't want to."

"The hell we don't," Karen said totally serious. "That was part of the pact. Damn, I wish I could find my copy. We all signed it, you know. We would sport our achievements. We would tell about any real failures. Then we would state our hopes and plans for the future."

"Okay, okay," Annette said. "I don't think we thought this through very well thirty years ago. But if that is what you all want to do--"

"It's what we said we would do," Karen said. "It was part of the plan."

"Okay!"

"Okay."

"Until tomorrow."

Chapter 22

Pancakes and Pals

None of the four women really wanted to go to the Pancake Supper. They wanted to hide away in their rooms and think about the afternoon. But each had made promises to go, and go they would. Annette went with her brother and family, and Stacy went with her niece. Paula and Karen decided to go together and promised to leave if the event got too boring.

Irene Crawford was sitting inside by the door when they arrived. She looked slightly embarrassed, and they quickly saw why. A sign by the ticket taker said "Irene Crawford Benefit."

"Hi, Irene," Paula said with a smile. "It's good to see you. How are you?"

Irene managed a smile, but it was strained. "I have a chemo treatment tomorrow. I'm always nervous the day before that. And this," she said with a wave of her hand. "I mean I don't want to appear ungrateful. It's very nice that they are doing this. But--"

"It kind of puts you on the spot," Paula said. "But people care and want to help. This is one way we can."

"I know," Irene said. Then her voice lowered, "Everyone is so helpful and supportive. I should be ashamed."

"Of course, you shouldn't," Karen said. "Listen, there's no reason for you to sit here on display. Come on. We're going to find a table. Then we're going to load up on pancakes and sausage. Where's Mark? I'd love to see him again. He and one of my brothers were in the same class. I can't remember which one. Brother, I mean."

Paula, Karen, and Irene sat at a table in the corner. Irene ate little but her spirits seemed to improve as Karen kept up a continuous chatter. One by one, Irene's five children made their way over to check on their mother and to meet her old schoolmates. It wasn't until almost eight o'clock when the supper was to end that Mark joined them.

"Had last minute business to take care of," he said and bent down to kiss Irene. "Pancake's any good?"

"You're welcome to mine," Irene said and pushed the plate toward him. "They're probably cold though."

Mark didn't seem to mind. He stabbed a big bite with the plastic fork and crammed it in his mouth. That bite wasn't fully chewed and swallowed before another bite went in.

"You didn't eat lunch again, did you?" Irene said. "Mark, I've asked you not to skip your noon meal. We can't have you getting sick, too."

He shook his head and gulped some juice. "Too busy. You know how it is. Hey, is that…oh, hell, what's her name?"

They all looked toward the door.

"Annette Thackeray," Karen said.

"That's her," Mark said as he finished up the pancakes. "Yeah, I saw her and her husband doing an interview on TV one night. That old boy she's married to makes some sense. We'll, I'll be damned! Is that Stacy Winters? I used to have such a crush on her."

"All you boys did," Irene said, not at all perturbed with his revelation. She handed him a napkin. "Karen, go see if Annette and Stacy can come over and say hello, would you, please?"

"Sure." Karen jumped up and took off.

Paula shook her head. "Wish I had her energy. I had almost decided that Annette and Stacy weren't going to make it. And I knew they were planning to come."

The women walked to the table and exchanged greetings and hugs.

"You're late," Paula pointed out.

Annette grimaced. "Wouldn't you know the governor's office called just as I was leaving? They want me to attend a brunch next week to announce a new wing on the University of Texas campus. Then I had to reach Brent to make sure I could get out of another commitment. I need a social secretary. Anybody interested in the job?"

"I would be," Irene said. "I'd love to do something like that."

"Maybe someday," Mark said and stood quickly. "Got to go see Hank over there. Watch my girl for me, will you, ladies?"

Irene bit her bottom lip and looked away. "He never wants to talk about the future."

"It's okay for him to be afraid," Stacy said. "You, too for that matter. I want to apologize for my being late. Nina's kids had to finish homework, and then we had a flat halfway here. But if you'll save me a seat, I'll go get some of those pancakes now."

The rest of the evening passed quickly. The Fearless Foursome got reacquainted with so many old friends, they began to feel like they had never been away. They were joyous when they saw the fire chief hand Mark and Irene a check for over nine hundred dollars.

"Remind me to quit bitching so much," Karen said as she and Paula pulled into the parking lot of the Leisure Inn. "Just looking at Irene makes me feel like the luckiest lady alive."

"I know," Paula said with a sigh. She locked her car doors and headed for the building. It had been a long time since she had felt so old and tired. And so very, very lonely.

Chapter 23

Hanging Out

Part One – Paula

Paula was waiting in the parking lot on Wednesday when Claire pulled up. They enjoyed an hour of pleasant conversation on the way to the beauty parlor. They were early, but the beautician was ready for Paula.

"And what are we doing today?" she asked Paula, her voice and smile way too perky for someone as introverted and conservative as Paula.

"I need a trim," Paula said.

"Yes, you do." The woman, whose embroidered name on her blue smock read "Candi", ran her fingers through Paula's hair and scrunched it several times. "Definitely need a cut. And thinning. Too much bulk here. How about a little coloring to take care of that mousy look? And maybe you would like for Loretta to give you our complimentary facial."

"No, I--"

"Give her the works!" Clair said. "This is a gift from me and her brother. Pamper her! I have some business to do for William, but I'll be back in time for my appointment."

"Don't you worry," Candi said. "We'll take good care of her. You won't even know her when you get back."

Paula straightened in the chair. "Wait a minute. I don't want anything too drastic. I want to know me when you get finished. I just want--"

"I have just the cut in mind. And the right color, too. Oh, this is going to be so much fun!"

"But I--"

Paula might as well not have been there had she not been the guinea pig. She watched helplessly and silently as her hair was snipped and dropped to the floor. While Candi was timing the coloring, ("don't worry, it washes out in a few weeks,") they turned her chair away from the mirror and Loretta proceeded to rub lotions and all sorts of things on Paula's face. She tried to ignore the nagging sense of dread. What if she looked like some sort of freak when they were done? What if she looked so bad that she didn't dare show her face for the rest of her visit? What if she looked like Karen?

That, Paula thought, was unkind. That wild, daring, radical look worked for her friend. But it just wasn't Paula. Paula closed her eyes and resigned herself to the inevitable. All she had wanted was a simple trim.

"There!" Candi whirled the chair back so Paula could see herself in the mirror.

Paula gasped.

"And if you like the makeup, we can offer a sample starter set with all the colors we used for only $34.95. And there are coupons for your next purchases. There is enough foundation and lotions to last at least a couple of months. The lipstick will last much longer than that," Loretta said. "I've written the best colors for you on this card and Candi will put the hair color down, too. What do you think?"

"Oh, my gosh," Paula said, her voice a whisper.

Her hair, which had been a drab brown, was now a bright golden brown. Where it has been a simple shoulder length, her hair was now short and feathery. The makeup was stunning. Her eyes were vibrant and the shape well-defined. Her cheeks had just enough color to giver her a healthy glow. And the lipstick made her lips shine enticingly.

Paula had expected a dramatic change. But not this!

"Now, honey, tell me what you think," Candi said as she reached over to fluff the hair above Paula's ears.

"She's gorgeous," Loretta said. "You just have to get this makeup. It works for you. I'll give you some samples, too. Play around with it. See what makes you feel good. You want the kit? You can't beat "34.95.""

"I can't afford--"

"Very low maintenance hairstyle," Candi said. "It brings out all your best features, too. What do you say, honey? You like it?"

"I...I'm stunned," Paula said. "It's certainly different."

"Oh, it's different. But it's a great look for you," Candi said.

"See what I'm doing to it right now. Just wash blow dry, and fluff. You can use a curling brush if you want a little more height. But don't mess with any of those nasty gels and mousses. Keep it natural. You better get that makeup from Loretta. It takes about ten years off."

"I really can't afford--"

"Holy moly! Paula?"

Paula, Candi, and Loretta all turned to Claire who stared in amazement.

"It that you, Paula? Great Scott! You look younger than me!"

Paula looked at her sister-in-law, smiled, and looked up at Candi and Loretta.

"I'll take it," she said.

While Claire was getting her hair done, Paula walked down the street peering into the various shops. But the only one she entered was Dollar Daze where everything was a dollar or less. Paula liked stores like this because sometimes she got name brands so much cheaper.

She felt like she was floating. She was still in shock over her new look, but it made her feel like she hadn't felt in a long time. She couldn't explain it. She was vital; she was special. She was alive.

Dollar Daze impressed her. Their merchandize was good stuff. She found small wicker baskets in various shapes that were cute and practical. Paula thought about how fun it would be to fix a gift basket for Annette, Karen, and Stacy to give them Sunday before they all said good-bye. She chose three baskets and then decided to do a thank-you basket for William and Claire as well. Taking her time, she looked the store over and finally decided on food items for William and Claire plus a nice lotion. She also chose the lotion for each of her friends as well as little address books (hoping they would take the hint), a candle with holder, a tube of bath oil beads, a pretty scarf, a small book called *Friends to the End,* and a bar of chocolate. Each basket would cost eight dollars, and Paula was already worried about the thirty-five dollars she had spent on the cosmetics. But it would be worth it. It would be fun to put together and fun to give. She hoped it would be fun for Annette, Karen, and Stacy to receive.

Paula was headed for the check-out when she saw Irene Crawford and a pretty girl about seven months pregnant enter the store. Paula wheeled her basket toward Irene.

"Irene! Good morning! Well, actually almost noon, isn't it?"

Irene looked at her for a moment, and then her eyes widened in recognition.

"Paula? My goodness. You look much different than you looked last night. You look wonderful. Oh, I don't mean you didn't look good last night. I just meant...well, you are stunning today."

Paula blushed, wondering if she had let herself go so badly that she looked much worse than she realized.

"Thank you. My sister-in-law decided I needed a haircut."

Irene grinned. "That's one thing I don't have to worry about right now." She touched the turban on her head. "But I'm saving a fortune on shampoos. Paula, this is my daughter-on-law Courtney. We just stopped for a minute so Courtney could get some pencils and some treats for little Landon. He's in kindergarten. I think this is the second bunch of pencils we've had to buy. They must really use them a lot."

"I think it's more likely that they let the kids sharpen their own," Courtney said. "As I understand it, it's a game to see who can get the lead the sharpest. Excuse me. I'll just pick up a few things before we get Mama home."

Paula watched Courtney waddle off, envying her. She had loved being pregnant. She had loved carrying the baby and bringing it into the world. Nothing else had ever been as fulfilling and satisfying. She was meant to be a mother if not a wife.

"You've already had your treatment?" Paula asked. "You look good."

Irene grimaced. "It will hit me about the time we get home. Then I will be wiped out for the next two days. I think I'll go back to the car. You really do look lovely, Paula."

Courtney had already gathered her purchase and headed for the checkout. Paula waved her ahead. While she waited, Paula turned back to see Irene fingering one of the scarves with a hint of a smile. Then she picked up a cute little porcelain figure of a cocker spaniel and touched it to her nose. Paula was surprised at the gesture and the tears that sprang into Irene's eyes.

"Look, Courtney. Doesn't this remind you of Millie?"

Courtney nodded grimly. "Yes, Mama. You want to go to the car? I'm about done here."

Irene placed the dog back on the shelf and walked out of the store without a word. Paula watched and then turned to Courtney, her eyebrows raised in a silent question. Courtney shrugged.

"Millie was Mama's dog. She died a couple of months ago. She was fifteen. Dad had given Millie to Mama for Christmas when Millie was only six weeks old. It was a hard loss. Millie always stayed right by Mama, especially after Mama had chemo. I have to go. It was nice to meet you."

Paula nodded but found the lump in her throat was too big to speak. She nodded for another shopper to go ahead in line. Then without daring to give herself a chance to worry about cost, Paula whirled the basket around. She grabbed the scarf Irene had been looking at and the little dog figure. She picked up another wicker basket, more lotion, another candle set, bubble bath in a champagne shaped plastic bottle, a chocolate bar, and another copy of the book on friends. Then she firmly pushed the basket to the check out and never even flinched when the clerk asked for the grand total of $42. 83.

Part Two – Stacy

Stacy couldn't remember the last time she had slept so long. It was after 9:30 when she finally came awake, stretched, and realized the morning was almost gone. She hurried to get a shower and dress before thinking about coffee. There was a note on the kitchen table when she walked in.

"Aunt Stacy, I'll have a surprise for you at lunch. It will be a little late as I don't get off work until noon. See you then. Nina."

Stacy shivered with giddy excitement. How could the simple word "surprise" encourage so much anticipation? She made her bed and straightened the den. Then just before noon, she made her daily call to Daniel. To her relief, he sounded quite well.

"Will Perry be having dinner tonight with you and Austin?" she asked. It was a standing date that her nephew, the one she had given a kidney, dined with them on Wednesday evenings.

"Oh, yes," Daniel said. He hesitated and then added, "I believe he said someone else would be joining us. We're to meet at the Sizzling Steakhouse at six."

"Someone else?" Stacy was intrigued. Did Perry finally have a girl friend? She and Daniel had teased him about it enough times.

"Yes," Daniel said. "A good friend, I guess. I'll tell you all about it tomorrow."

"Is the writing going well?"

"Very well, dear. But I am anxious for you to proof it for me. You know how I value your opinion."

Stacy smiled. Daniel was not only a gifted writer but quite skilled in grammar and spelling. He definitely did not need her, but she loved being part of his work.

"Oh, darling, I hear Nina pulling in. She said she has a

surprise. I can't image what it is."

"I'm sure it is something you will enjoy," Daniel said. "I'll speak with you again tomorrow, my dear. That is, unless you want me to call you this evening."

She did, she did! She hardly could wait until Saturday when Daniel and Austin would be joining her. "How about I call you? I'm not sure when the girls and I will break up tonight."

"Until then, dear. Do enjoy your surprise. I love and miss you."

"I love and miss you, too," she said. Even she caught the wistfulness in her voice.

"It's only two and a half more days," Daniel said and laughed. "Go now. See to your surprise."

Stacy replaced the phone and felt tears sting her eyes. She was such a baby. Here she was, a middle-aged woman who was so homesick she could hardly stand it.

"Aunt Stacy! I've brought you a surprise," Nina said behind her.

Stacy placed a smile on her face and turned around. Her mouth dropped open.

"Raelene!" She ran across the room to embrace her oldest sister. "Oh, Rae! When did you get here? I had no idea! Will you be here for the weekend?"

"No, no. I don't care anything about school homecomings. I'm just here for a couple of hours. Then I'm off to see Perry."

"Perry? Then you're his mysterious dinner date. Daniel knew

you were coming, but he didn't mention it!"

"I knew you were here," Raelene said, "And I thought it would be fun to surprise you. But I am on a mission. So I'll be leaving soon. I'll try to stop again as I come back through on Friday. Now let me look at you."

Nina smiled at her two aunts and gathered up her car keys.

"Aunt Rae, it was wonderful to see you. I'm going for groceries, so I'll leave you and Aunt Stacy to visit. Do stop back on Friday. We'll be counting on you to do that."

After Nina left, Raelene and Stacy sat at the table to eat the deli sandwiches Rae had brought. Their conversation was about family and the upcoming homecoming weekend.

"Tell me, little sister. What in the world are you going to do with all that money when you get it?"

Stacy stared at her. "Oh, Rae! I don't have any idea that I'll get the money. Annette and Paula and Karen have all done so much! You wouldn't believe their accomplishments."

Raelene took a deep swing of soda and set the cup down hard.

"Nothing any of them did can be greater than you giving a kidney to Perry."

Stacy smiled. "Not to you, Rae. But Karen and Paula have both saved lives. And done so many other things."

"So you don't think you'll get the money?"

"I don't know. I don't even care, if truth is to be told. It has been so good to see the girls again. But I miss Daniel and Austin something horrible. Now why are you driving across the state to see Perry? Wouldn't it have been easier to fly in to the Dallas-Fort Worth Airport?"

Raelene's sober look alerted Stacy that something was not right.

"Rae?"

"I've been driving because I've also made stops to see Christy and Kathy," she said referring to her two daughters. "I wanted to talk to each of them in person."

Stacy's heart pounded. Something was wrong.

"Rae? Are you all right? What's wrong?"

Her sister put a trembling hand to her mouth. Stacy reached to take her sister's hands in hers.

"You're scaring me. What is it?"

Raelene took a deep breath.

"It's Carl," she said referring to her husband of forty-two years. "He's just been diagnosed with lung cancer. All those years of smoking. It's advanced. He's been sick off and on for a couple of years but I couldn't get him to the doctor. But he came down with pneumonia this last week, and the cancer was discovered."

"Oh, Rae." Stacy's voice was barely a whisper. She could not bear to think of the pain her sister was experiencing. How would she herself deal with the prospect of losing Daniel? He was older than her siblings and their spouses, but thankfully his health was good except for being susceptible to bronchitis.

"I'm telling the kids one by one in person. It's hit the girls hard, of course. And I don't think it will be any easier for Perry."

"And they're saying Carl doesn't have a chance?"

Raelene shook her head. "No. He probably didn't anyway, it's so advanced. They're afraid it has spread to other organs. They'll be running more tests on Monday. That's why I have to get back. They only give him a couple of months, Stacy. The doctor's aren't even sure he'll make it to Christmas."

They cried and clung to each other. Stacy had never been that close to her brother-in-law but liked him. She was very close to her sisters though and their pains were hers.

"I would give anything if I could fix this for you," Stacy said in a whisper.

Raelene nodded and sniffed. "Like you did for Perry. But this time you can't. I'm just trying to prepare myself and help Carl face it. And I have to be strong for the kids. You know how close they are to their daddy."

Stacy didn't know anything of the sort. She had always been under the impression that Carl subscribed to the belief that children should be seen and not heard. But it wasn't her place to voice such negative thoughts, especially now.

They talked for another hour before Raelene said she had to get on the road again to Perry's. It was almost a four hour drive if the traffic wasn't bad.

"I thought I would like to stop by the cemetery and see Mama's and Daddy's graves," Raelene said as she gathered up her purse and jacket. "Would you like to go, too?"

Stacy had planned to go to the cemetery while she was in

Bonnetville but hadn't found the time. She had been dreading the visit. But it seemed right that she and Raelene should go together.

"Yes," she said. "I'll follow you in my car. You'll be on the right road out of town and won't have to worry about coming back here. And I can go directly to my meeting with the girls."

"Sounds good," Raelene said. Her voice was flat and dull and Stacy wondered if anything would really sound good to her sister again.

They stood looking at the graves of their parents who shared a headstone with the names and birth and death dates. Stacy watched as Raelene brushed aside twigs and dried grass.

"They've been gone a long time," Raelene said.

Stacy nodded.

"I miss them almost every day."

Stacy was ashamed. To be honest there were days at a time she never thought of her parents. Her life was wrapped up on her own family now.

"If I miss them every day after they've been gone so long," Rae said, "how in the world am I going to get over losing Carl?"

Stacy wrapped an arm around her sister. "We'll all help. And I like to think that he won't be that far away. You're strong, Rae. I've always counted on your strength. You'll handle it. But I promise you won't have to do it alone."

They stood holding onto each other, looking at the headstone and sobbing quietly.

"We live, we die," Raelene said.

"And we live again," Stacy said. "And while we live, we make the most of what we've got. That's so important."

Raelene placed her head next to her sister's.

"You've always given me so much joy, Stacy. From the moment you were born, you have meant the world to me."

"And I've looked up to you and relied on you far more than I should have."

"Nonsense. I deserted you when I graduated. And now I've got to get on the road. I'll stop back in for a few minutes on Friday. But I want to get home. Carl has those tests on Monday, and I need to be there. Right now, his sister Aggie it staying with him."

"Drive carefully," Stacy said.

"I will. You enjoy the rest of your visit, and I'll give Daniel and Austin big hugs from you."

Stacy laughed though it was weak. "Do that. But I'll be so glad when I can give them in person."

Raelene rolled the window down in her car and looked out at her sister.

"Sometimes it is the pits loving people," she said.

Stacy nodded. She waved as Raelene drove off.

And sometimes it was all that made life worth living, Stacy thought as she headed to her own car.

Part Three – Karen

Karen pulled up in front of the nursing home and shoved the

gear into park. Without thinking, she pulled a cigarette out of the package on the dash and pushed in the car's lighter. In seconds, she was drawing deeply and exhaling. Then she snuffed out the cigarette and ran her fingers through her hair. Why did she ever get started on the nasty things? She didn't like smoking; it was a filthy, vulgar habit.

Why was she procrastinating? This was her father, not some demonic dictator she didn't want to see. Grabbing her purse, she almost tumbled out of the car in her haste to go inside. She did not want to back out, but she also very much did not want to go in.

Head high, she marched into the building and down the hall to her father's room. It was empty. She retraced her steps to the reception area but did not see him sitting in front of the television set where the aides so often left him. Confused and slightly alarmed, she went back to his room. It was neat, clean and clinical. There was only one ancient family picture on the table by the bed. Karen must have been about eight years old when it was taken. How differently they all looked! What happened to that tall, dominating man who sat beside his wife and was surrounded by seven children? What happened to the little girl who looked like she owned the world?

Where was her father? A sudden, paralyzing fear swooped over her. What if...no that could not happen. The people here knew she was in town. Her father couldn't have...no, someone would surely have called her. And her brothers would have been notified. But where was he? She rushed up and down the halls looking in every direction but saw no sign of Claude Montgomery. Finally, she hurried to the office and pushed her way through the door.

"Where is my father?" She was breathless and panicky. "I can't find him anywhere."

The administrator and her secretary looked up from the computer they were studying.

"Mrs. Brewster, isn't it?" the administrator, Mrs. Pollack said. "You father is Claude Montgomery."

"I know who my father is," Karen said in her most snappish tone. "What I don't know is where he is."

Ms. Pollack came around the desk, gently took Karen's arm and escorted her out of the office. "I'm sure he's nearby. Sometimes the aides take him outside."

"Not today," Karen said, still peevish though beginning to calm down. "It's way too cool for him to be out."

"Then I'm sure we can find him." Mrs. Pollack stopped at the front desk and picked up the house phone. "Glenda, could you tell me where we can find Mr. Montgomery. Thank you. Please do check."

Mrs. Pollack kept the phone to her ear, but turned back to Karen. "I assure you your father is fine. We rarely misplace our— Yes? Thank you, Glenda."

The administrator replaced the phone. "Your father is being given a bath. That does tend to take awhile. Would you like to wait in the reception area? Could I have some coffee sent to you?"

Karen's face went from ghostly white to deep red.

"Thank you," she said though Mrs. Pollack may not have been able to understand the mumble. "I'll just…be right in here."

Karen sat and grabbed a magazine to fan her face. There was nothing like making a fool out of yourself first thing in the morning. A middle-aged volunteer appeared with a white foam cup of coffee.

"Here you are, dear," she said. "If you would like some reading material, someone donated this box of old magazines. I can't imagine why. These are about celebrities or mechanics or other subjects that our residents don't really care about. But you might find something to pass the time."

Karen thanked her and sipped the coffee which was among the worst she had ever had. Grimacing, she set the cup aside and picked up a magazine on top. It opened to a page and Karen found herself looking into the very handsome face of actor/director/writer Jace Collins. He was one handsome man, Karen thought. Those blue eyes alone gave her a thrill.

Karen flipped through the pages but decided that Jace Collins was the most interesting read. She read the sidebar first. "Why Jace has decided that acting is no longer as satisfying as it once was. Jace takes a bigger role in writing the screenplays. What older woman has won Jace's heart? What is Jace's most romantic date?"

"He can date me," Karen said to the magazine. "With those eyes and dimples, I'd follow him anywhere."

Sighing, she started the article. But it wasn't until she got toward the end that she really paid attention. She paid so much attention that she knocked the coffee over and had to grab tissues off the table to wipe it up. Then she once again picked up the magazine.

"Jace Collins is one of the most eligible bachelors in all movie land. Once married for two years to actress Heidi Phillips, Jace has lived quite a solitary life for the past five years. "I concentrate on my work," the thirty-seven year old actor told us. "I was raised in a small town in Mississippi by hard-working parents. I was taught Christian values and good manners. Most people think I would be better suited to another line of work. But I happen to like to act, and I do it well." But will he remain celibate for the rest of his gorgeous life? Jace chooses not to discuss his relationships. But close friends have confided that Jace Collins is very smitten with an older woman, a writer of award-winning children's books whom he met on a talk show last year. When we asked him about this love interest, his only comment was, "She is exactly the type of woman I always hoped to marry." We wonder if he is serious enough to ring those wedding bells. If so, many hearts out there will break as another mega-hunk takes himself out of circulation."

Older woman? A writer of children's books. Could it be? It had to be Paula! But why in the world was she keeping this dreamboat a secret? Karen would have been shouting the news to the world.

Looking around to see that no one was watching, she carefully tore the article out of the magazine, folded it, and slipped it in her purse.

"Here's your daughter, Mr. Montgomery!" An aide pushed the wheelchair toward Karen and turned it toward her. "He's all bathed and shaved and ready for a visit. But I have to warn you. He tends to get sleepy about this time."

"That's all right," Karen said. "I won't stay long. Hello, Daddy. How are you today?"

Claude Montgomery nodded his head slightly and licked his lips. They looked so dry that Karen dug lip balm out of her purse and applied it to his mouth.

"Got to plow that field."

Karen stared at him. "No, Daddy. You don't have to worry about the field."

Her answer agitated him. He shook his head, clearly annoyed and slapped the arms of the wheelchair. "Can't wait! And the cow has to be milked."

Karen took his hands in hers and rubbed them with her thumbs. "Okay, Daddy. I'll take care of it."

"See that you do!"

"I will."

Whatever lucidity there had been now faded, and her father stared into the distance. Karen spoke to him gently even after he fell asleep, his head dropping down toward his chest.

"I promise not to fall asleep if you hold my hands like that."

Karen jumped and looked up. Ryan Wardlow grinned.

"What are you doing here?"

He offered a hand and pulled her to a standing position. "My Aunt Caroline has been living in the assisted living side. But she's beginning to show signs of dementia, and they want to move her on this side. She'll hate it. But she can't do much anymore, and we can't have her being a danger to herself and others. I was just signing the papers. I'm her legal guardian since her daughter died." He looked at her dad and then back at her. "It's not easy, is it?"

"No."

"Going to be here long?"

Karen sighed. "No. There's no use in me staying." She signaled to the aide that came over. "I guess you better take him back to his bed," Karen said. "This can't be comfortable for him."

"Don't you worry," the aide said. "We'll take care of him. I'll get Vincent to help me put him to bed."

"Thank you," Karen said her voice barely above a whisper. She bent over to kiss his wrinkled cheek. "Bye, Daddy. I love you."

Karen and Ryan watched them push her father back down the hall. Ryan watched Karen for a moment and then took her hand.

"Hey, how about some lunch? I've got a one o'clock appointment back at the office, but a body has to eat. What sounds good?"

Karen was about to tell him that she wasn't hungry and should get back to the hotel to meet the girls. But those words refused to come out. Instead she answered, "Tacos."

Ryan grinned. "Now that's a can-do. I know just the place. Should I drive, or do you want to follow me?'"

Karen slipped her purse strap over her shoulder. "I'll follow. I want refried beans and rice, too."

"Yes, my lady. What's that?"

Karen looked at the cigarette in her hand. She hadn't even realized she had taken it from her purse.

"This? A nasty little habit I--"

"It certainly is."

Ryan snatched the cigarette from her and tossed it in the trash can as they walked past.

"Hey!"

Ryan held the door open for her. "Hay is what we feed horses."

Karen slipped in the car and reached for the seat belt. "I just don't like bossy men. That is going to cost you dessert, too."

Ryan pushed the door closed and leaned down to stare in at her.

"Lucky for you, I can afford it."

"Lucky for you, I agreed to eat with you."

"Lucky for you I asked."

"Lucky for you I didn't want steak and lobster."

"Lucky for you I don't kiss you right here in public."

Karen started the motor and shifted into gear. "Lucky for you I'm going to beat you there and get to pick the place to sit. Pablo's

Casa, right? I've seen it every day I've been out. I know exactly where it is."

She left him laughing and racing for his pick-up truck.

Part Four – Annette

Annette punched "end call" on the phone and swore quietly. There weren't a lot of people she disliked, but Claudia Bronson was one of them. She was Brent's secretary, and he liked her. And Annette had to admit that Claudia, who was nearing sixty, was very efficient and took good care of Brent.

She slipped her sweater from around her shoulders and pulled it on her arms. She would have to go in soon. It was getting much cooler, and the clouds gathering overhead threatened rain. But it had been pleasant sitting out by the pool alone taking care of some of the business that had become her responsibility over the past several months.

The phone trilled its ridiculous ringtone her daughter had programmed in and she snatched it up and jabbed the button.

"Yes? This is Annette. Oh, Clyde. How are you, Mayor? Yes, I know I've been selected as Coming Home Queen. It's an honor," she made a face, "but one I hardly deserve." No one deserves this crap, she thought. "Don't you think one of the other girls--?"

She broke off as the mayor interrupted her. "Thank you, Clyde. That's very kind. But--"

She held the phone away and bumped her head against the

table a few times while he raved on. Sighing, she gathered a deep breath and broke in.

"Then Clyde, I have a stipulation. As queen, I should have a royal court. I choose Paula Clifton, Karen Brewster, and Stacy Durfey as my ladies-in-waiting or whatever. We were the top four in our graduating class. We've all been high achievers. And I absolutely refuse to accept this honor unless you honor them, too."

Paula walked up and took a seat opposite Annette.

"I'm sorry, Clyde. That's my final offer. They must ride in the convertible with me, or I won't be doing it. I can't help that there won't be enough room for Gilbert. Perhaps he can have his own car as Director of the Alumni Association. I'll talk to you later, Clyde. Thanks for calling."

She tossed the phone down and stared at Paula. "What have you done?"

Paula jumped and looked around with a guilty expression. Then she touched her hair.

"Oh. Claire's idea. It looks okay, doesn't it?"

"Okay! It looks fabulous. But it's not just your hair. Something else is different. New lipstick?"

Paula smiled and shifted self-consciously in her seat. "New everything. I guess I'm a sucker."

"Sign me up. Oh, here comes Karen and Stacy."

The other two women took seats at the table. They both looked at Paula and then did a double take.

"Paula!" Stacy squealed. "You said you were going to get a

trim! You look adorable."

Paula grinned. "It's what happens when they won't let you look in the mirror."

Karen helped herself to cake crumbs on a plate in front of Annette.

"You look divine, darling," Karen said in an exaggerated drawl. "Like a movie star. Or a movie star's wife."

Paula looked at her quickly and Karen returned her stare without blinking. Paula swallowed hard and turned to Annette.

"What in the world were you talking about when I walked up?"

Annette sat up straight. "Oh. Guess what I found out. Gilbert Hathaway is scheduled to ride in the car with me when we ride around the football field at halftime."

"Giblet Gilbert?" Paula's mouth fell open. "You cannot be serious."

"Oh, yes," Annette said. "The committee even called Brent's office, and his psycho secretary gave me a quarter hour lecture on why I must endure such torture for the sake of my husband."

"Nuts." Karen licked her fingertip and pressed it against the remaining crumbs. "Old Gibby's had a crush on you since third grade. Let your husband make the sacrifice this time."

"I agree," Paula said. "I hate to be judgmental...I do so, Karen! Most of the time. But the term big, fat slob--"

"Big, fat, smelly slob--" Karen said.

"The point is," said Paula, "no. You do not have to do it. So that's that."

Stacy laughed. "What if he's changed? What if he's slimmed down and taken a bath in the last thirty years?"

"He hasn't," said Annette. "He was at the function at the mayor's house the other night. He's about three hundred fifty pounds and bathes in some sort of after shave I'd never be able to identify. And he's married. His wife probably weighs over two hundred pounds. They are quite the pair. And he kept making excuses to touch me. Innocently, of course. He would put his arm around me or reach over to pat my hand. I can't help it. The guy still gives me the creeps."

"So it's settled," Paula said. "He can't ride with you. Period."

"Oh, good!" Annette clapped her hands. "Then you will all do it!"

Karen, Stacy, and Paula exchanged looks.

"I missed something," Stacy said.

"Me, too," Paula agreed.

"Spill," Karen demanded of Annette.

"You'll be my princesses or ladies-in-waiting or whatever, and you'll ride in the convertible with me."

"I don't want to ride in a car around the football field," Paula said. "No way."

"I'll be with Daniel and Austin," Stacy said.

They all looked at Karen. "Hell, I think it would be a hoot." She waved to an imaginary audience. Then she gave a regal nod to a pool toy that floated past.

"You'll do it?" Annette gave a sigh of relief. "Thank you, thank, you, thank you."

"Only if these two yahoos do it, too," Karen said.

"Please!" Annette burst out her pleas before Paula or Stacy could protest. "Please! Please! Please!"

"You know you're missing out on a good political move here," Paula said thoughtfully. "You should have Brent ride with you. In fact, you should have Brent announce his candidacy on Saturday afternoon and then ride in the car with you. It would be a great photo-op. Go for it, girl!"

Annette shook her head. "I don't know that Brent is ready to announce yet. But there would still be room in the car for Gilbert. I want you three and Brent, too, if he will. Us with the driver…well, no way, Mr. Hathaway."

Paula, Stacy, and Karen grinned at each other.

"Oh, come on!" Annette said. "You owe me."

"Who owes you," Karen demanded.

"All of you. Remember our senior year when you three sneaked out of the English class window and ran down to the store across the street for candy. I was on hall duty and could have gotten you put in detention. But I turned the other way."

"We went out the window, not down the hall," Karen protested.

"And besides, we gave you part of the candy," Paula said. "So we're even."

"Please!" Annette made the word sound desperate. "Do you

want me to get on my hands and knees?"

"Just your knees," Karen said. "That will be sufficient."

Annette shoved out of her seat and started to kneel, but the other three were on her and laughing before she ever touched the concrete. Like schoolgirls, they clambered around, giggling. It wasn't until they heard a nervous clearing of a throat that they quickly resumed their seats and made a pretense of decorum. A young man from the hotel staff stood uncertainly before them. He held the largest fruit basket either of them had ever seen.

"Good gravy! How much does that thing weigh?" Karen said.

"It's pretty heavy," he admitted. "It's for Mrs. Clifton. Shall I leave it here or take it to your room?"

Paula grabbed the card before Karen could get it. "Take it to Mrs. Thackeray's room. That's where we're headed right now before it starts raining."

"Dibs on that pineapple," Karen said as the rain started coming down in quick heavy drops. "And I want to see that card, missy."

"What card?" Paula asked as she slipped it in her purse.

Chapter 24

Confessions

They settled in Annette's room, and Karen and Paula sliced fruit and set it on the table. They made conversation, repeated themselves, ate, went to the bathroom, remembered phone calls they had to make, and did anything they could to keep from getting to the task at hand.

"We really don't have to do this," Karen said and stuffed a chunk of pineapple in her mouth.

"Yes, we do. Even you said so yesterday," Stacy said and reached for a slice of mango. "That was part of the contract we signed thirty years ago. We tell our accomplishments. We confess anything we've done that might take away from what we achieved. We tell what we hope to do in the future."

"Nobody has seen that stupid contract since we signed it," Annette said sounding irritable. "We can do what we want now."

"No, we can't," Stacy said.

The other three looked at her, and she pulled a worn folded sheet of paper form her pocket. Unfolding it with care, she laid it on the table for them to see. It was the contract, and it was signed by all four of them.

"Shit," Karen said.

"Trust you to have a copy," Annette said.

"Why trust me?" Stacy folded the paper again. "I'm the one who always lost things, remember?"

"So why have you got this?" Karen crammed a bite of banana and some peach in her mouth. Juice oozed down her chin. "Why is this the one thing you managed to not lose?"

"Because I thought it was something we were totally serious about. I thought we had every intention of following through."

Paula eased away from the others and took the card that came with the fruit out of her purse. She slipped it out of the envelope and smiled as she read, "Sweets for the sweetest. I know how you love fresh fruit. Alaska is incredible. I want to bring you here soon. Love Jace."

"Would you kindly let us know who the hell your secret admirer is?" Karen's voice was almost a yell that caused the others to jump. "What the hell is so important about keeping his identity a secret? I know who he is anyway."

Paula's face burned, and she turned away to replace the card in her purse and to blink back tears.

"Oh, Karen, you do not," Stacy said.

"I do. Don't I, Paula? Shall I tell everyone?"'

Paula squared her shoulders and turned back to face them. She was flushed, but her voice was controlled though soft.

"Maybe you do. I wouldn't put it past you though I don't

know how you could. But I would prefer that you kept the knowledge to yourself. If you don't mind, please. I agree with Stacy. As a matter of fact, I have a copy of the contract in my purse too, if you would like to see it. But if you're really uncomfortable doing this, then keep your mouth shut. Just shut up! I plan to follow through just like we discussed years ago. Remember the reason we planned it this way? To encourage us each one to do our best and to remember that we depend on each other for encouragement and support. Stacy, since Annette and Karen obviously don't want to participate in this part, I suggest you and I continue on as planned."

Stacy nodded. "I...I'd like to go first."

"Why you?" Karen snarled. "Why can't I go first?"

"You don't want to do it at all," Paula pointed out.

"I didn't say that! I just said--"

"I would like to go first," Stacy repeated.

"Why?" Annette spoke for the first time since they mentioned the contract.

Now Stacy was the one to turn a deep shade of red. "Be...because I don't want to back out. What I have to say...I want to clear the air. I want to...I don't want anyone thinking that I am better than I am. I...I mean I try to be good. I really do. But I did something that has a direct bearing on why we are together this week. Once you hear what I have to say, you may think I'm not deserving enough for the money to even be in the running."

"You?" Paula laughed. "Come on, Stacy. There can be

nothing that bad. Not from you."

Stacy was crying now. She grabbed a tissue from the box by the bed and dabbed her eyes. "You won't think that once I've finished telling you. But I have to do this. I've waited all these years to confess and hopefully make amends."

"This bad, awful, horrid thing you've done," said Annette. "Does anyone else know about it?"

"Yes. Daniel knows. I told him before we ever married. And he knows I plan to tell all of you this afternoon. He doesn't think it is necessary since I've tried to correct the mistake I've made, but he supports me in my decision to do it."

Paula sat on the edge of the bed away from the others. Her voice was low and shaky. "It can't absolutely can't be worse than what I have to tell."

"I swore I would never tell something," Annette said. Her voice was thoughtful and she seemed to be thinking. "I told Brent if we were to be honest this week, I would have to tell. He doesn't want me to. Bad political move if it ever came out. Can we vow right here and now that whatever comes out in this room today will never leave this room?"

"I don't care if it leaves," Stacy said. "I plan to tell the proper people anyway."

"If it just affected me," Annette said, "that would be one thing. But it could hurt Brent and the kids. It would hurt my parents. It would hurt all of them."

"I agree with Stacy that what I have to tell doesn't have to be kept absolutely secret," Paula said after some thought. "But I really would hate for it to get out either. It…it wouldn't be good for me. Or my children."

"What about *him*?" Karen asked, her tone snide and accusing.

Paula looked her in the eye. "It wouldn't be good for him either. But he does know about it."

"Look," said Annette. "Can we sign another one of those damn contracts? I've got my laptop and printer right here. Can we write up something that says we will never divulge the information we hear today? If we choose to discuss our own experience, that's fine. But we cannot ever talk about what the others confess."

"Can we trust each other enough for that?" Karen asked.

"I trust you all," Paula said. "If you tell me you won't share what I have to say, I trust you. I'll accept your word. We don't have to sign anything."

"Yes, we do," Karen said. "Write something up. Make the copies. I'll sign."

"And you have something to share, too?" Paula asked.

"Yes, dammit. Is that good enough for you?"

"And it's that bad?" Paula asked.

"Bad enough."

Annette pulled her laptop on the table and quickly typed out, "I, (name), solemnly swear to never discuss any information imparted on this day and time. Should I do so, the other signers are free to deny all and any accusations and risk suffering the loss of trust and friendship. Those offended may unite against the betrayer to protect and preserve their own privacy and well-being. We do agree to refrain from discussing any information given this day with any other person outside the four signers below."

Annette printed out four copies, signed them, and shoved the copies to the center of the table.

Paula took up a copy and read it. She laughed and Annette bristled.

"All right, you write it. I'm not the writer here. We hire people to do our writing."

"Oh, Annie, it's no big deal," Stacy said as she read over Paula's shoulder. "It's just kind of funny and cute the way you worded it. I'll sign." Stacy took the four copies and quickly scribbled her name and date. She then offered the papers to Paula.

Paula looked them over carefully. "I'll sign," she said. "But I think it is important to honor the part about not discussing it with anyone else. Only the person who shares her...uh...past should be able to tell it to anyone else. I know you, Stacy, and you, Annette. You tell your husband everything. This is one time you can't."

"I'm the one who wrote it," Annette said.

"Okay." Paula signed all for copies and slid the papers across the table toward Karen.

Karen looked at them but didn't sign. Instead she picked up some grapes and popped them into her mouth.

The other three exchanged looks. Paula shrugged.

"That's okay. If you don't want to do it, that's fine. But I don't think you have any right to stay and listen to the rest of us."

"Shut up! Shut the hell up!"

Karen grabbed the sheets of paper, signed very slowly and deliberately, took one sheet, folded it, and put it in her purse by the door.

"I want to go first," Stacy said.

Part One – Stacy

"You seem awfully eager to spill your guts," Karen said and bit into another slice of peach. "Must be because you have so few sins that--"

"Karen, would you please just shut up and listen?"

It was so unlike Stacy to interrupt that the other three stared at her in amazement. She took a deep breath and continued.

"I hope – really, really hope – that this won't change the way you feel about me. Oh, it will of course. I'm fooling myself if I think it can't affect your opinion of me. But please, please try to understand. I was so young and stupid. I was desperate. I was willing to do almost anything to go to college. I wasn't as smart as the rest of you, so I had only one very small scholarship. It wouldn't have helped me even through the first semester."

"What's she talking about?" Karen asked and looked around at the other two. "Does anyone know what she's talking about?"

"Shut up," Paula said.

"Please, listen! This is so hard. Mama was so sick, and I hated that. I loved her. But I didn't want to be stuck in this hokey little town and become an old maid. Or else marry someone just because he was available. I had really high hopes and lofty dreams."

"We always knew you wanted to be a teacher," Annette said. "You wanted that from around the fourth grade. But I never realized there was any question about you going to college. I thought that was the plan all along. And that your mother would move to El Paso to be close to your sister, the nurse."

"That's the lie I lived that whole last year of school and the summer after graduation," Stacy said. "I could not face the possibility of not going to school, of not becoming a teacher. Of not meeting someone who would sweep me off my feet and solve all my problems. Of course, that didn't happen anyway. My first husband caused more problems than I ever imagined could exist. And Daniel didn't exactly sweep me off my feet. And he hasn't solved all my problems. But he has helped me work through them and make them bearable."

"Whatever it is you're not telling us," Paula said, "does Daniel know about it?"

"Absolutely. I told you I told him before we were married. And I told him that I was going to tell all of you today. I wouldn't do anything without consulting with him first. And I'm trying to tell you if you'll just listen. This is so hard! Please, don't keep interrupting."

The other three sat conspicuously silent and watched her, waiting. Stacy took another deep breath.

"I was desperate. I was stupid. I knew it was wrong, and I've regretted my actions every day since. I regret it even after I tried to right the wrong."

Karen started to speak and was gouged in the ribs by Paula.

"You remember the money that was stolen from the bank the end of summer after we graduated? It was a big deal because that bank had never had a robbery in its eighty-four years of existence. You remember that?"

Annette, Paula, and Karen looked at each other wondering if they were permitted to speak now. Not taking any chances, they merely nodded.

Stacy nodded, too.

"I took it."

The combined gasps of the other three shattered the quiet of the room, and Paula blurted out, "You couldn't have!"

"I did."

The tears welled up on Stacy's eyes, and she blinked fiercely to hold them back. But instead, they trickled down her cheeks. Impatiently, she wiped them away with her hand.

"It was two thousand dollars. But that was a lot of money back then. It more than paid for tuition and books for my first year of school."

"But how--" Annette shook her head to clear the confusion. "You weren't working there anymore. I remember that clearly because Mother made a comment about how lucky it was you were gone so you didn't have to face the accusations and suspicions the other employees had to go through."

Stacy cringed at the thought of putting others into awkward and embarrassing circumstances.

"Let me explain. This happened on a Wednesday evening though it wasn't discovered until sometime Thursday. My last day had been the Friday before, so technically I wasn't still employed. But Mr. Griffin had three tellers out on that Wednesday. At the time, there were only three tellers besides me. But one had had a minor car accident that morning heading to work. Another had a gall bladder attack and had to go to the hospital in Cullen. I forget why the third one had to leave early. But Mr. Griffin personally called and asked if I would go in and cover for the last three hours. He said he would pay me double. I wouldn't have refused him even if he hadn't paid me at all. He was a dear man, always so good and sweet to me. And I had to repay him by being a thief!"

"How could you possibly get away with doing something like that?" Paula asked. "You were the biggest coward of all of us. You were always afraid of skipping school or staying out past your curfew."

Stacy shook her head. "I don't know. I couldn't do it now. I'd have a heart attack just thinking about it. But I was so desperate then. Mama and I had had a talk over the weekend. She said she couldn't pay for any of my college because she just didn't have the money. I thought there was some of Daddy's insurance money left. I knew my sisters had both received a few hundred dollars from his policy, and I assumed I would too when I got ready to go to school. But Mama told me she had had to use it to buy groceries and clothes and pay the utilities. You know, just to keep us going. Mama hadn't been able to work that much for a couple of years, so the money ran out. Of course, I worked on Saturday for two years. But that was only four hours at something like three dollars an hour. I worked two summers but that didn't add up to much. And I had to pay for the rental on my graduation cap and gown and buy my announcements. I thought I had to have a senior class ring, too, like everyone else. Mama couldn't buy any of that so I did. Oh, I was so stupid. So stupid!"

Annette got up from the chair and sat by Paula and Karen on the bed.

"I got one of those silly rings, and I never wear the thing. I only wore it a few times that first year I was in college. I don't even know where it is anymore."

"I pawned mine with anything else I could come up with for money to get me and the boys away from Todd," Karen said. "Never missed it. Never even thought about it."

"I didn't get one," Paula said. "I couldn't afford it. And I figured I would be wearing a wedding ring soon, and that was a lot more important."

"I wish I hadn't bought one," Stacy said. "I lost the darn thing down a pipe in a hotel in Mexico when my government class took a weeklong trip there. I don't even know why I was wearing it."

Stacy wiped her face with both hands and looked up at her friends.

"So there. You know my secret. I've never done anything so

horrible again. I've been almost fanatically honest. If someone gives me even a dime too much change, I go back to return it. If I find I wasn't charged enough for something, I point it out. I've gotten really obsessive about being honest, so I guess I did learn something from my crime."

"But how did you do it?" Paula asked. "How did you pull that off?"

Stacy answered. "It was easy really. Mr. Griffin, Mrs. Creighton, and I counted the money at the end of the day and balanced out everything. Mrs. Creighton was the administrative assistant. We had all the money from the cash drawers in the bins to take to the vault. We left it sitting on the counter just at the vault's entrance. Mr. Griffin paid me cash for my time, wished me good luck, and escorted me to the door. Then Mrs. Creighton called to him that he had a phone call he had been expecting all day, so he rushed back. At that time, his office was downstairs. I could hear him calling to her to join him on the other line. They thought I was gone. But I was standing at the door wondering what I had forgotten. Then I realized it was my umbrella because it had been raining most of the day. I went back and got if off the hook in the lounge area. As I was going back out, I saw the money still in the bin. I looked around, grabbed several of the stacks, stuck them in my purse and left. Just like that. My heart felt like a jackhammer going off in my chest, and I was sweating all over. I didn't even know how much I had taken until I got home and counted it. Two thousand dollars even. I walked the floor all night worrying about what I had done."

"I had decided to take the money back to the bank and confess. But Mama came into my room early the next morning and told me she needed me to drive her to the hospital. On the way, she kept telling me I should badger Mr. Griffin into giving me a full-time permanent job and a promotion. That pretty much decided things for me. I knew Mama would try to run my life from then on. I had to escape. But I promised myself, I would pay that money back and make up for what I'd done."

"Did you?" Karen asked.

"Did I what?"

"Did you pay it back? Did you make up for taking it?"

"Yes. And yes. Yes to both questions."

They waited but didn't ask the obvious. Stacy shook her head.

"All right. I paid the money back and more. I think I put back something like thirty-seven hundred before Daniel put his foot down and said I had punished myself enough, But I never regarded it as punishment. I also put more into our fund when I could. And as I said, I have tried very hard to be the most honest person possible since then. I've done pretty well there, I think."

"So the bank knows you were the one who took the money?" Annette watched Stacy carefully.

Stacy blushed and showed renewed nervousness. "No. No, I don't think they could possibly know it was me. I...I sent cash each time and never put my name on anything. I just sent a note the first time saying I had taken the missing two thousand dollars and would be paying it back as I could with interest. No, the bank couldn't possibly know it was me."

Karen leaned forward to stare into Stacy's eyes. "Are you going to tell them?"

Stacy swallowed so hard, they would hear her. "I have to, don't I? I mean, I think I had planned to at some point. The confession isn't complete otherwise, is it? Oh, lord!" Her breaths became short and rushed. "I wish Daniel was here. What should I do? I have to tell, don't I? Oh, lord. Can they arrest me?"

Annette made a face and shook her head. "I doubt it. I think the statue of limitations is probably long past. You've repaid the money. You've never done anything like that again. I doubt you ever will. It's not like you think you can get away with it any time you want to."

"I never want to do anything like that again! If I hadn't felt so trapped and desperate...believe me, I learned a valuable lesson. But I...I think I need to tell someone. Davis, maybe? I probably need to talk to Davis."

The silence was so long, Stacy stared at each of her friends.

"Oh, please, try to understand. I know I let you all down. But I had to tell you. I should have told someone years ago. Daniel is the only other person on this earth who knows."

Annette took Stacy's hands in hers. "Hush, you goose. Do you really thing we don't love you anymore? Come on, Stacy, you haven't even heard our confessions. This may be bad to you, but I guarantee mine is far, far worse. So much worse, I'm not sure I can even tell you. I'm still trying to get up the courage. I know the person you are. I know what you've done in life since our childhood. You're still the sweet, kind loving person you always were."

"Who just happens to be a thief," Karen said.

Stacy gasped but then relaxed when she saw Karen's wicked grin.

"Thank you, Annette. I…I appreciate you for not judging me. I promise I won't judge you either."

"You can count on me, too," Paula said getting up to hug her. "We all signed that paper, so if you don't want this to go any farther, it won't. But if you decide to tell Davis…well, I for one will go with you."

"You would do that for me?'

"Of course. Just remember though. We need your support, too. I don't know about Karen and Annette, but I'm going to spill my guts. And it's not pretty either. I would be happy if I had just been guilty of a little theft. Especially a theft I had paid back."

"I'll go with you, too," Karen said. "I mean if you decide to tell Davis, I'll go. He's still as cute and cocky as he used to be."

Annette grabbed a pillow and pummeled Karen about the head and shoulders.

"You idiot!" she said as Karen dodged and reached around to grab a pillow of her own.

"Okay, okay! Truce!" Paula yelled. "Knock it off, you middle-aged delinquents. We need to get done here. If Stacy's confession was so hard, we have a lot more to get through."

Stacy smiled at her, Annette, and Karen who finally tossed the pillows back on the bed. Her relief was so great, she felt a love for her friends that she wanted to embrace forever. The burden of sin was now gone so that she felt physically lighter. It was wonderful.

"I seriously doubt any of you did anything worse than what I did," she said with a smile.

Paula sobered and plopped onto one of the straight-back chairs around the table.

"How do you feel about murder?"

Part Two – Paula

Paula studied the floor frowning as though she didn't like what she saw. Once she shook her head slightly like she was arguing with herself. Only when Karen made a production of clearing her throat did Paula seem to remember she was not alone in the room. She jumped and gave them a guilty-looking grin.

"Oh, sorry. Did you say something?"

"No, we did not say something," Karen said with irritation.

"You left us speechless," Annette said.

"You didn't really, did you, Paula?" Stacy watched her with wide eyes and a slightly horrified expression. "You didn't really...you know...murder someone."

"Oh. Well, no. Not really. But I honestly did try. I chickened out though. Had a change of heart. He did get good and sick, and I've never felt real bad about that. Considering...everything. At the time. I mean, it seemed justified. To be honest, I didn't really think of what I was doing. Too much television of cozy mysteries, I guess. Maybe. Something like that. I don't know."

Karen and Stacy stared with disbelief mingled with confusion. Annette sighed deeply and settled back on the bed to make herself more comfortable.

"You need to start again, Paula," Annette told her. "Who did you try to kill?"

"And why?" Karen asked.

Paula's chin quivered and she bit her bottom lip. "Gary. I tried to kill my husband. At least, I wanted to kill him if only for a brief time. It...it was the night of Lilea's funeral. I...I was devastated. I...I couldn't believe that she was gone. My beautiful little girl. The three older kids had gone back to the motel with my sister Jana Sue. There was a pool, and they really needed to get away. They all loved Lilea so much. And being so much older, they had helped care for her and teach her. It was so hard on all of us. Well, not all of us. Gary had never wanted another child, and he was still resentful that I had brought her home in the first place. But he had gotten used to having four children. And there were times Lilea gave him the social upstanding he enjoyed. Anyway, the kids were with my sister. I was looking for Gary to see if he wanted to eat. We had tons of food people brought in. I finally found him in the den. He was on the phone with his friend Walter. Those two...they're the best of buddies. Have been for years. They're both bigots and idiots. Anyway, I overheard Gary tell

Walter that we had had to bury the chink that day, and he was sorry that Walter hadn't been able to make it to the funeral."

A collective gasp brought out a sob from Paula, but she continued.

"Then Gary laughed like he had just head the funniest thing in the world. Here I was feeling like I would never smile again, and he is laughing like an idiot hyena. And he had called Lilea, my precious baby, a chink! Something in me snapped. I swear to God I didn't even think. I just went into the kitchen and prepared a plate for Gary. A very special plate. I spiced it with rat poison."

"Uh-oh." This was from Karen.

"Oh, yeah," Paula said and nodded. "I didn't want to use so much that he would taste it, but wanted to use enough to make him good and sick. I guess I wasn't really thinking about killing him. I just wanted him to suffer like I was. I thought, at least in my mind that night, I thought it was justice. I really did."

"Did he eat?" Stacy asked.

"Oh, yeah. He ate. He said Mrs. Palmer's lasagna tasted funny. But he ate it. Within an hour, he was throwing up something awful. I've never seen anyone that sick. I guess it jarred me back to my senses because suddenly I felt so bad about what I had done. So I tried to help him feel better. I gave him medicine and soft drinks and kept wiping his sweaty forehead with a cool, moist towel. It was almost dawn before he stopped throwing up. But he didn't feel good for several days. He always blamed it on Mrs. Palmer and her lasagna."

"You never told him, did you?" Stacy asked.

Paula shook her head. "Nope. And I'm never going to. If he ever learns about it, it will be from one of you."

"Not me," Karen said. "You should have given him a little more."

"Karen!" Stacy turned her horrified gaze on her friend. "You can't mean something like that."

"Hell I can't. The guy is a jerk! He didn't even care that his daughter was dead because she was something other than what fit into his perfect little world."

"But still--"

"She's right," Paula said. "Gary has always been one who cares how things look to the rest of the world. When it made him look good to have adopted a little girl from China, he was pleased to play the daddy bit to the hilt. But when it made him look bad to his racist friends, she was always my child."

"Dirt bag," Karen muttered. "Never did like that guy."

"Okay," Annette said. She had been strangely quiet and withdrawn. "So you did a horrible thing, but it turned out okay. You probably were out of your mind with grief. I'm sure you didn't know what you were doing. Or at least, you weren't responsible for your actions at that time."

"But if he had died," Paula said, "I would have been charged with murder. And no jury would have cared about anything except I had killed him."

Annette nodded thoughtfully but didn't speak.

"Anything else?" Karen said.

Paula shook her head. "I guess not. That was bad enough. By the grace of God, I'm sitting here with you tonight instead of a jail cell."

"Well, it didn't happen so let's go on. Are you sure there isn't anything else?"

Paula gave an irritated growl. "Honestly, Karen, wasn't that bad enough?"

Karen held up her hands as though to protect herself. "I'm just saying…well, if that's all that's happened in thirty years--"

"Oh."

"Oh, what?"

Paula grimaced. "Well, there was one other incident I can think of. It wasn't anywhere near as bad as poisoning Gary. But it wasn't nice, and I've regretted it ever since."

"Go on," Karen said and sat back by Annette. She fluffed a pillow behind her and stretched her legs out on the bed.

"Okay, you ghoul. I was in a nice store in Amarillo. Can't even think of the name now because I've never been back. But I had Rick and Lilea and Lilea's little friend Natasha. Natasha was a sweet little black girl, and she and Lilea were best of friends. We went to this store to get Rick some sneakers. His feet are funny, and he can't wear the cheap ones long because they don't provide enough support. So I had the three kids, and we were trying to find the shoes he needed. Anyway, there was this woman who seemed to be everywhere we were in the store. She kept looking at us.

Finally, when she was admiring a bracelet at the jewelry counter, I heard her tell the clerk to look at us. There were three kids with three different fathers. She was giving me such dirty looks."

"You should have ignored her," Stacy said.

"I know. But I couldn't. I gave her my best evil eye and told her in the frostiest tone possible that not only did they have three different fathers, but they had been borne by three different mothers. The clerk was mortified. But the woman just threw up her head and turned away. She put the bracelet back on the counter and stomped off. I was so angry. I always get mad if anyone messes with kids, especially my kids. Well, this woman was wearing a coat with huge pockets. I picked up that bracelet when no one was looking, walked right past that busybody, and dropped the bracelet in her pocket."

"Oh, no," Stacy said.

"Oh, yes. Then I calmly paid for Ricky's shoes. The woman was just finishing up her shopping at another register so she got to the door before we did. Oh, my gosh! The buzzers all went off, and there was the most awful racket. Three or four security people literally swooped down on this woman. She was so embarrassed she was almost crying. They searched her and found the bracelet. They immediately rushed her upstairs and called the police. The police arrived before I had the kids buckled up in the car."

"That was mean," Karen said. "Stacy's right. You don't give in to jerks like that. You set her straight. You should have let it go."

"Oh, great," Paula said. "Who are you to judge? I was angry. She had no business trying to hurt my kids. I didn't even think. I just did it."

"You're pretty good about setting up people to look like thieves, aren't you?" Karen said.

Paula's face reddened. "What do you mean by that?"

"In high school. Do you think we didn't all know? You set up Shirley Walker. You're the one who took Mr. Gleason's watch off the counter where he always left it while doing the science experiments and put it in Shirley's purse.

"Karen." Annette's voice was warning.

"No! We all knew about it. Maybe if we had said something then instead of all agreeing among ourselves that it was a lousy stunt to pull, she wouldn't have done it again as an adult."

Paula trembled. "How dare you? That was in high school and it has no relevance to what we are doing today. And if you knew, you should have said something. You were supposed to be my best friends."

"We knew how badly you wanted to go to the junior prom with Brian Kellogg," Stacy said. "You and Davis had just broken up, and everyone thought Brian was going to ask Shirley. If Shirley hadn't always been pulling dirty stunts on everybody else, we would have said something."

"She pretty much deserved anything she got," Annette said. "Karen, you should be ashamed. You know we agreed then not to ever mention it."

Karen sat back, arms folded, a stubborn look on her face. "I know it. And I wish I had kept my mouth shut. But when she told about that lady in the store, it just sounded so much like with Shirley that...all right. Forget I said anything."

"Oh, I'll definitely forget it." Paula's voice was thick with sarcasm. "You were always so perfect, weren't you?"

"Paula, Karen, please," Stacy was close to tears. She could never bear to see her friends fight and their actions today brought back less than happy memories.

"I never said I was perfect. I wasn't perfect. I am not perfect," Karen said.

"You always had everything you wanted. You got away with everything. It was like you were charmed. You were the perfect little everything."

"I had six older brothers who made things work for me. I had a father who thought that I was the whole reason for the earth's existence. Believe me those days didn't last long enough. I've had to struggle and fight ever since. It's something I've gotten good at."

Paula cupped her face in her hands and tried to control a sob. "I'm sorry," she said in a whisper. "I'm so sorry. I don't know why I lash out at people when I get angry or scared. You're right, it was a really crappy thing to do to Shirley. And if it gives you any satisfaction, I had an absolutely horrible time with Brian. Maybe I can locate Shirley and apologize. It's not much, but it's all I've got to offer."

Annette shook her head. "This is one sin you'll have to live with. Shirley was killed in a car wreck several years ago. What happened to the lady in the store?"

Paula took a deep quavering breath. "I couldn't go through with that any more than I was able to go through with killing Gary. After I saw the police go in the store I went down the street to a pay phone. I called the store and asked to speak to the manager about a robbery. Of course, he answered immediately. I told him the woman with the bracelet was innocent. I had dropped the bracelet in her pocket. Then I hung up before he could ask any questions. And like I said, I never went back to that store again."

"You make a terrible criminal," Karen said.

Paula gave her a rueful look. "Not for lack of trying," she sighed. "I'm good at failure though."

No one spoke for several long minutes. Finally, Annette said, "Is there anything else? If you're finished, we might want to take a break for dinner. I would like to treat you to barbecue in Cullen."

"That...that's all I can think of," Paula said. "Of a serious nature anyway. There have been lots of times I've not been a particularly nice person. But those are the two times that I regret the most."

"Barbecue sounds delicious," Stacy said. "I'd like to help pay."

"Nope," Annette said. "This one is my treat. Let's go. We'll resume when we get back. At least, I will. What about you, Karen? Anything you want to share?"

"Sure," Karen said as she slipped on her shoes. "I'll tell you how my ex and I swindled folks out of five hundred thousand dollars. Think they'll have cornbread? Cornbread sounds really good."

Part Three – Karen

Karen refused to say another word until they had driven the eight miles to Cullen, loaded up on barbecued beef, pork, sausage, and chicken, corn-on-the-cob, beans, coleslaw, fried okra, and cornbread and driven back to the motel. They waddled their way to Annette's room, groaning and whining about being so full.

"I can't believe I had to pass on that coconut cream pie," Karen moaned. "I never want to see another bite of food as long as I live." She waved toward the fruit basket, now pretty much depleted and said, "Get that thing out of my sight!"

Paula sat the basket on the dresser by the door, and Stacy went down the hall for a bucket of ice. When she returned, she filled four plastic cups with ice, added water, and set them around. Then she settled in one of the chairs at the table across from Paula. Annette and Karen resumed their casual claim on the bed.

"I'm ready," Stacy said. "What were you saying about swindling five hundred thousand dollars?"

"She's joking," Paula said. "She's just trying to outdo us." She was grinning, but she watched Karen closely.

"Yeah, right," Karen said. "Like I want to be the worst one here. But here's the story. My ex, my last ex Nick

Brewster...hummm, where to begin. We went into business together when we married. He and I were both established accountants, and we had a nice little office at the back of our house. I was happy keeping books for a dozen firms and individuals, advising them and helping as I could. But Nick...well, Nick always wanted more. And he loves to take risks. He – and I don't know how he did this – but he talked me into using some of our client's money to make investments. He was going to use the money and not say anything to them. But I wouldn't agree to that. So he talked to each client and convinced them that he would increase their assets, guaranteed."

"Guaranteed?" Annette had been listening with her eyes closed but now she opened them and looked at Karen.

"Yes, the idiot guaranteed it. I wanted to have each client sign a waiver saying we were not accountable, if you'll pardon the pun, for any investments that did not pay off or did in fact lose them money. But Nick wouldn't hear of it. Of course, I didn't know he had already guaranteed them a profit. So he took different sums from all the clients and made investments. Some were so obscure, I'd never heard of the companies. Anyway, only two paid off to any degree. Again, unknown to me, Nick paid those two clients double of what they had invested and put the rest in our account as a commission. But the other ten who lost...well, some were significant. Anyway, we suddenly found ourselves owing them thousands and thousands of dollars. Since he had guaranteed a profit, we had to liquidate something fast to at least cover the amount they had invested. Then we had to come up with some fast cash to make it look like they had made something."

"When was all this?" Paula wanted to know.

"Two and a half years ago. After six months of juggling the books and selling off some of our own assets, I was feeling pretty frazzled and a lot frustrated. That's when I found out that Nick had also invested our savings. All of it. Over fifty thousand dollars. And lost every cent. I could see that we were going to be in big trouble if we were audited, but Nick didn't seem to care. One day, I got a call from one of the clients wanting to know where his twenty-five thousand dollar profit was. He wanted to spend it on some land in Montana, and the bank couldn't find any record of it. Of course not. Nick had lied to him. I confronted Nick. I showed him the books and got him to tell me exactly what he had promised and to who. Whom. Whoever. Well, to make a long, sad scary story short, we owed over five hundred thousand dollars. We had no money to speak of, but we did have our house and my vehicle. Nick's BMW had to go, and I think he actually cried. He had to settle for a plain old Town Car though it was new and loaded. I was afraid that he was going to get us both thrown in jail. Anyway, I filed for divorce. I got the house and found him a nice two bedroom townhouse down the road. He went back to work for the company we had left, and I made sure he gave me five hundred dollars a month to apply to what we owed our clients. I also made sure he paid child support even though he wanted the girls every other week. So he's not living too high off the hog these days. Tough. I found a job in the accounting department of an oil company and kept working for the twelve clients I had. Most of my salary goes for living expenses and the girls. But I have been able to put away a bit each month to build back a savings. I've made a couple of sure thing investments for our clients but nothing too risky. We're gradually getting our clients paid back, all the while hoping they don't catch on. And praying they don't all want their money at the same time."

"What about the one who wanted his money for land in Montana?" Stacy asked.

Karen sighed heavily. "That took more juggling. I took it from another client. Now I've been trying to get that repaid before they want their money. It's been a nightmare. I think if we got caught, the courts would see me as guilty as Nick though I had no knowledge of what he was doing at first. And I've tried like hell to get it straightened out. Once we're square with everyone, I am finished completely with Nick. I'll never do another bit of business with him, I don't care what."

"How much do you still owe everyone?" Paula asked.

Karen grimaced and then shrugged. "Less than a hundred and fifty thousand. Not that bad considering it's been only a couple of years. But I live in constant fear that everyone will want their money at the same time. That we will get caught and lose everything ourselves. I have no doubt we would both end up in prison.

"Then the money in our fund--"

"No!" Karen's voice was harsh and she shot a spiteful glare at Paula. "I would never accept that money for Nick's embezzlement. He deserves to pay and pay through his teeth. Besides, that's not what that money is for. It was never to get any of us out of trouble."

"I agree," said Annette as she sat up. "But I think we would rather change our rules than see you go to jail."

"No way." Karen's teeth were clenched, but the words were crystal clear. "That money will go to the most deserving, just like we planned all along."

"Okay," Paula said. "It was just an idea."

"A crappy one."

"All right!" Paula pressed her lips together to control the tremble. "Just trying to be a friend."

"Or show us up," Karen snapped back.

"Paula, Karen," Stacy said, pleading. "Please".

Annette took a big sip of her ice water and set the cup back on the table by the bed.

"Okay, you could be in big trouble. No doubt about that. But you're working to correct it. I wish you all the luck in the world. If for some reason, you find yourself in a position where you can't handle it, let me know. I do have some influential friends. Promise me, you'll do that. Karen, stop looking so obstinate. Promise me!"

"Okay! All right. For my children, I promise that much."

Annette nodded. "And even though I know you wouldn't like

the idea, I can lend you the money. Lend, not give," she stressed when Karen started to protest. "At whatever interest rate you like. And now as you're been saying, anything else?"

Karen scratched her head and looked around the room as though trying to see more sins etched on the walls. "Aw, hell. Yeah, there's something else. I swore I'd never tell anybody this, but I guess I might as well come as squeaky clean as the rest of you."

"Up to you," Annette said. But she didn't sound like she meant it. She sounded like she hoped Karen was finished.

"What is it?" Stacy asked warily. She had been glad to clear her conscience, but she was growing weary of hearing everyone else's burdens.

"I had an affair."

"Just one?" Paula asked.

"Damn you!" Karen sat up straight, eyes flashing and fists clenched. "I am not a slut or a tramp, Miss Goody-Goody. I'm also not a frigid little prude who is afraid to show her feelings for a man."

"Karen, I didn't mean…fine! I'm a prude. Go on. Let's just get this over with. I'm tired. I've had enough."

It took awhile for everyone to settle and relax again. The tension in the room was stifling. But finally, Karen spoke.

"It was a guy I met at work. We were out most days doing audits, so we were together a lot. He was fun and good-looking, and it was easy to sneak away each day. Ron and I--"

"Ron!" Stacy's protest was a howl. "But I thought that was the husband you really cared about! I thought you said that marriage would have lasted if he had lived."

Karen turned a cool gaze upon her. "I did love Ron. But he wasn't the most passionate of men. And I am a very passionate woman. It just happened. We didn't plan it. We were both married, and we wanted to stay married. It was wrong, but we did it. After six months, he transferred somewhere back east. We agreed that it was over and it was best to end it completely. I've not seen or heard from him since. And it's been years."

"Did Ron ever know?" Paula asked.

"No."

"Thank God," Stacy said.

Karen rose up again but Annette put out a restraining hand.

"Okay, embezzlement and an affair. Anything else, Karen? Are we ready to move on?"

Karen sat back grudgingly. She wanted a good fight. She had wanted a good fight for two years now. But Nick was not a fighter. A thief and a spendthrift, yes. But a fighter, no.

"There's one other thing I've never been too proud of. After I left Todd, I refused to let his parents see the boys. I didn't trust them especially Todd's father. It would have been just like them to take the boys and hide them from me. I never had a doubt of that."

"So the boys never saw their grandparents again?" Paula asked.

"Why do you keep asking me what I've just told you?" Karen said.

Paula shrugged. "Just want to make sure we have the facts straight."

"Todd's dad never saw the boys again. His mother visited us a couple of times on the sly. I let her see the boys so long as I was there, too. And the boys had strict orders to never, under any circumstances, go with their dad or grandparents. I lived in fear that Todd would appear at their school and take them. I didn't have anything legal that said he couldn't have them. I thought I was protecting my sons. And I was. But I was also being spiteful. I was paying Todd back for being so cruel to us. His mom died about four years after I left. Three years after I took the boys, Todd left a bar and rolled his pickup. He was paralyzed from the waist down. One day, he got his father's gun and shot himself to death. He thought death was better than not being a whole man. I never let the boys know that. I didn't want them to live with the stigma of having a father who committed suicide. They always regarded Ron as their father anyway."

"Sad," Stacy murmured.

"Sure as hell wasn't," Karen said. "He deserved everything he got."

"But still--" Paula started to say.

"Still nothing," Karen said snappishly. "He got what he asked for which wasn't nearly as much as he dished out."

"You're not telling us everything," Annette said. "You're not telling us everything Todd did to deserve your wrath."

"And I'm not going to."

Annette nodded. "Fair enough. Do you have anything else you would like to share?"

"Don't you think that's enough? I could go to jail for stealing, to hell for having an affair, and to the woodshed for depriving my children of their grandparents. Can you beat all this, Mrs. Thackeray?"

Annette sighed and rubbed her eyes.

"I'm afraid I can."

Part Four – Annette

No one moved or spoke. It was inconceivable that brilliant, sophisticated, charming Annette Thackeray could have done something even more atrocious than the three others. Annette had had it together since first grade. She always knew what she wanted and she didn't stop until she got it. She knew how to manage people, and she knew how to take care of herself. Paula, Stacy, and Karen waited, hardly breathing, eager to hear whatever Annette considered a bombshell.

But Annette didn't speak either. She sat back against the pillows, legs extended, eyes closed, and a pained look on her face. One by one, the other three realized that Annette hadn't said much while they were 'fessing up'. It slowly began to dawn on them that maybe Annette too had something troubling from her past, something that she would rather not share or divulge.

"Come on," Karen said. "How bad can it be? Especially compared to what we've just told you. What happened? Did you vote twice in an election?"

Annette smiled, eyes still closed. "No."

"Try to kill Brent?"

She shook her head.

"Stole money? Maybe from the great State of Texas?"

Annette opened one eye and turned it toward Karen. "You are an idiot. All right, I'm going to tell you. There are only three other people in this world who know. Brent and my parents. That's it. This could greatly hurt Brent and his campaign if it got out. It would hurt my kids. I never want them to know. It would hurt my parents. It would hurt me. Again. This has been buried for over thirty years. If it ever surfaces, it will come from this little gab session."

"Oh, thanks a lot!" Karen got off the bed where she had been sitting next to Annette and took a chair between Stacy and Paula at the table. "We spill our guts and trust you to keep your mouth shut. But you think we can't be trusted? Listen, sweetheart, you're the damn politician."

"Karen," Stacy and Paula said at the same time.

"Knock it off," Paula added. Then to Annette she said, "Just tell us. If you want. It can't be worse than trying to kill someone."

"Trying is the key word, Paula," Annette said. "I actually did it."

Stacy's gasp was the only sound. Then Karen's, "What?"

Annette folded her hands as though in prayer and touched the tips of her fingers to her nose. "Just let me talk. Let me get through this. Then you can ask all the questions you want. Deal?"

Paula and Stacy nodded, and Karen said, "So talk."

Annette nodded, her hands still on her face. "It was the night of graduation. You remember a lot of the kids wanted to go to the lake and celebrate. Paula couldn't go because Gary and his family had come for the graduation. Stacy couldn't or wouldn't because she wanted to go back home to visit with her sisters. And her mom was really tired. Everyone was worried that she would pass out before Stacy and her family could get her home to bed. And Karen...I forget why Karen didn't go. But I went. We were all so happy and excited to be out of high school. We were looking forward to the future, and we were ready to party. I don't know who brought the booze or where they got it, but there was lots of it. None of us had had much experience drinking, but we learned fast. Finally, everything was gone and most of the kids left. I don't know how we all got home in one piece. As wasted as we were, it's a miracle there weren't serious car accidents. Anyway, I was finishing up a beer, which I never drink anymore under any circumstances, and Ernie Watson was still there, too, in his big old ancient Desoto. We were sitting on the hood of the car drinking and talking and laughing. Do you remember Ernie?" She looked at the other three who sat like stone fixtures.

"You don't remember him?"

"You told us to keep our mouths shut until you were finished,"

Karen said. "Just doing what we were told."

Annette gave an exasperated snort and looked like she wanted to say something nasty to Karen.

"I remember Ernie," Paula said. "Star quarterback when Davis wasn't."

"Do you also remember that he was black?"

"Was?" Stacy said. "Is he--"

"I don't know!" Annette waved a hand impatiently. "I don't know where he is now. But you do remember he was black. He was a fun guy, always cutting up in class. Not being a nuisance about it. He just kept things light and fun. Anyway, I don't know how it happened, but we ended up in the back seat of his car."

"Uh-oh," Karen said.

Annette shot her a menacing look, and Karen pantomimed zipping her lips.

"Yes, it happened. I lost my virginity in the back seat of that car with a boy I didn't know that well. I think it was a new experience for him, too. And considering we were both stinking drunk, it's a wonder either of us were able to pull it off."

"That's such a shame," Stacy said thinking Annette was finished. "The first time, every time should be special and wonderful and memorable in a good way. It should--"

"That's not all the story, Stacy. Please let me finish."

"Oh! I'm sorry. I thought…please continue."

"Well, as luck or fate or whatever would have it, I missed my next period."

"Uh-oh," Karen said in a low whisper.

Annette shot her another look and Karen reached down to retie her shoes.

"I hoped, prayed that it was just because of all the stress of graduating. But then I started experiencing morning sickness. I've never been so scared in my life. I didn't know what to do. I didn't know where to turn. I knew my parents would be what my kids call ballistic. I thought about calling each of you but realized there really wasn't anything either of you could do. I was so ashamed. I didn't want anyone to know. But I knew this wasn't a problem that was going to go away. I finally had to tell my mother."

"And?" Paula asked.

"She was wild. Oh, my gosh. The screams, the threats, the berating. She literally locked me in my room and told me I wasn't to talk to anyone. She called Dad to come home, and they talked for hours. In the end, they told me Mother and I would be going to New Orleans for awhile. There was a person there would get rid of my problem and nothing would ever be known here. Even my brother wasn't told the truth. They told him that since I had done so well in school and made valedictorian, Mother and I were going to take a girl's vacation."

"You went to New Orleans? I thought you went to some exotic island," Karen said.

"That's the story my parents fed everyone. We went to New Orleans. The day after we got there, Mother took me to a...I would call it a seedy area...and I had an abortion. It was awful. I didn't want to do it. I wanted to have the baby and put her up for adoption. No, Karen before you interrupt again. I don't know that it was a girl. I just felt like it was. The fetus was apparently much too small to know. Having the abortion itself wasn't so bad. I had plenty of medicine to wipe out the pain. And Mother personally examined the premises and equipment to make sure everything was clean and sterile. But after the anesthesia wore off, I was in horrible pain. For two weeks, I bled and hurt. Then it got better. But the mental, the emotional pain…that's never gone away. So you see, Paula, I actually did kill a baby."

"No, you didn't," Paula said, her mouth and voice tight in a barely controlled rage. "Your mother did. She had no more respect for you and your body than she does for those ornate statues decorating their lawn. She was always a controlling, manipulating--"

"Paula!" Stacy hissed.

Paula shook herself. "Oh! Annette! I'm sorry. I…I just don't think you should consider yourself a murderer when it was your mother who forced you to do it. She's the killer. She and the doctor who would do such a horrible thing."

Annette got up to pour herself a cup of water. She drank it down and then poured another cup.

"You don't have to apologize, Paula. I'm well aware of the bitch my mother is and has always been. I love her of course, but I've never respected her. She and I are very different."

"Thank God," Karen said.

Annette ignored that remark. "Mother has always been concerned about what looks right, what other people think. She could not have dealt with having an illegitimate grandchild. Then there is absolutely no way she could have accepted one of mixed race. To her, the only way to deal with the problem was to get rid of the problem. I always wished I had stood up to her. I should have. But I guess it was easier to give in. After all, I wouldn't have to worry about what I had done, and I could blame her for the abortion."

"Yes, I guess that was easier than trying to go against your mother," Stacy said. "We all know how strong-willed she is. You were still just a kid. It was too much of a burden for you to handle alone."

"Except that's it is still a burden today. I think about that unborn child almost every day of my life. Every time I see a child of mixed parentage, I wonder. I regret. I suffer. For a long time, I worried about being able to have children. I had problems after the abortion that I never had before. So before we got married, I had to tell Brent. In case, we couldn't have kids."

"What did he say?" Karen asked.

"It didn't bother him as much as I thought it would. I'm Pro-Life all the way. He tends to lean a bit toward Pro-Choice but he doesn't care that much either way. Too many of our voters are women of child-bearing age. He doesn't want to rock that particular boat."

"How does your mother feel about...you know...now?" Paula

asked. "I mean, do you think she has any regrets?"

"Oh, please," Annette said. She went to the closet and brought out the bottle of whiskey she had opened days before. She splashed a little of the liquor into her water and set the bottle on the table. "Mother has never mentioned it since. Never. It's like it never happened. She's nuts about Josh and Lydia, but she never considers another grandchild she didn't let live."

Annette took a sip of her drink and looked at the other three.

"So was that bad enough for you?"

"Yes," Paula said being her usual frank self. "But I still feel it was your mother who is to blame."

"Surely," Annette said as she resettled herself on the bed. "I could have refused. I didn't think I could then. But looking back, I had the right to refuse."

"Having the right to do something and actually being able to do it are two separate things," Stacy pointed out. "Your mother was determined."

"Also," Annette said as though Stacy hadn't spoken, "I imagine it was easier in the long run. The decision was made for me, and I could go on to college and pursue the dreams I'd had. Even if I had had the baby and given her up for adoption, I would have had to hide out for nine months. Mother wouldn't have allowed me anywhere near Bonnetville. As it was, she wouldn't let us come home until I was pretty well mended. She made me sit out by the pool for hours at a time to get tanned. After all, we were supposed to be living it up on the island and not hiding out in some motel in New Orleans. It didn't do any good. I still looked like I had been through a near death experience. Oh, hell. Now you know. If you have any questions, ask them now. I don't want this brought up again. Ever. Just as I won't bring up any of your indiscretions."

"Did Ernie ever know?" Paula asked.

"Hell, no! I think he was so drunk he probably didn't even know we had had sex. He certainly didn't know about the baby. And since there wasn't a baby, there was no reason for him to know."

Paula nodded. "You're right. Okay, anything else?"

The all snickered a bit. That had become their mantra. "Anything else?"

"You won't let me get away with one horrible incident? Annette rubbed her face vigorously with both hands. "Karen! Don't you dare light that cigarette in my room. On second thought give me one."

"You smoke?" Stacy asked. She grimaced. "Not you, too."

"Not usually, no. Just this one. No more."

Karen took a cigarette, held the light to it, and inhaled deeply. Then as she blew out the smoke, she tossed the package and lighter across the bed to Annette.

"The things don't taste as good anymore," she complained.

"Did they ever?" Paula asked.

Karen made a face and wagged her head from side to side. "I don't know. But they used to give me some satisfaction. Go on,

Annette. It's getting late. Let's get this over with. What else have you got to confess?"

"This isn't much better than the abortion," Annette said. She took a puff of the cigarette, made a face, and crushed it out in the ash tray. "I may have let slip once that a certain male politician was having an affair with another male."

"Wait a minute," Karen said. "That would have been Yancy Proctor! I remember that. It cost him the election."

"It cost him his career," Annette said. "And it was my fault. There wasn't a shred of truth. But he was pulling ahead of my candidate, and I couldn't have that. I needed my candidate to win so Brent would be in a position to run today. I've never been proud of that little stunt, and Brent was absolutely furious when he learned about it. He tried to undo what I had done, but it was too late. The press had a ball. It's the only real fight Brent and I ever had. It came near to costing me my marriage. I vowed then that I would never do anything that cheap and underhanded again. I'll do a lot to help my husband, but it will be honest and up front."

"I liked Yancy Proctor," Paula said thoughtfully. "He impressed me as being a really nice guy."

"He is a nice guy. And of course, that makes what I did even worse. Brent and I've tried to make it up to him over the years, but understandably he doesn't want anything to do with us. He's not sure what we had to do with his downfall, but he knew we...I...was involved. Okay, that's it. I'm done."

"Me, too," Stacy said and stood. "This has been so

depressing. I just want to go home and call Daniel. No, what I really want to do is just go home."

"Stick with us a few more days, Stacy," Annette said. "We're almost there."

Paula stood, too. "I'll walk you to your car, Stacy."

"Me, too." Karen snubbed out her cigarette and stood. "Goodnight, Annie. They say confession is good for the soul. We should all be feeling pretty good right now."

"Bullshit," Annette said as though wishing them a good day.

"Exactly," Karen agreed.

They were at the door when Annette spoke again. "You know, I've been thinking, and I really like your idea for Brent to announce his candidacy on Saturday. I'm calling him right now. Thanks for the suggestion."

Paula and Karen watched Stacy's taillights disappear down the road before they turned back to the motel. On the elevator, Karen hit the button marked two for her floor and then the one marked five for Paula's. Then the elevator stopped. Karen got off, but she turned back and held the door open.

"I really do know who your secret is."

Paula nodded and chewed on her bottom lip. "How do you know?"

"It was in one of those celebrity gossip magazines at the nursing home. Listen, girl. He sounds like he really loves you. If you love him go for it. Life's too short to spend it being miserable. If this guy treats you right and you feel like he's the one, don't let a stupid thing like age hold you back."

"I just don't want anything to mess up his career."

"He's a big boy. A big handsome, cute, adorable boy. You go, girl!" Karen stepped back and let the door slide close. Paula's last glimpse was of Karen standing in the hallway giving her both thumbs up.

Chapter 25

Spending the Money

Only Paula was waiting in the parking lot when Stacy pulled up. Stacy was disappointed that Karen and Annette were not going to the bank, too. She needed all the support she could get. But it was more than that, of course. She was afraid that her friends thought less of her now knowing what she had done.

It wasn't fair. She didn't think less of them and their mistakes had been pretty bad, too. But Stacy had always been told that one of her greatest assets was her capacity to forgive. Stacy didn't feel that Paula, Karen, and Annette needed her forgiveness, and she didn't hold their mistakes against them.

"Hi," she said as Paula got in the car and reached for the seat belt. "Just the two of us, I guess."

"Good morning. Yes. Annette has a full schedule. She got a call from Brent's secretary last night, and is she steamed! Not so much that she has this all day agenda as the fact that the secretary is so bossy. But she did say that Brent agreed to go ahead and make his announcement. They'll call a press conference at the school on Saturday afternoon. Oh, and it's official. We are ladies-in-waiting or hand-maidens or something like that. Karen was waiting with me to go, too. But she just got a call from the nursing home that her dad is running a fever and not eating. And he keeps talking about his princess. So she thought she better go check on him."

"Of course. Poor Karen. She puts on such a tough, brave front. But I know things get to her. What kind of day does the lunatic secretary have planned for Annette?"

Paula grinned. "Well, she was to talk to the high school government class at 9:15. Then she is guest speaker at the noon Chamber of Commerce meeting and luncheon. At two, she is speaking to her sister-in-law's ladies club. Sounds like a fun day, huh?"

"Humm," Stacy signaled and pulled into the bank parking lot. "Probably going to be every bit as much fun as mine. Oh, Paula, I am so scared! Let's get this over with."

They barely caught Davis Griffin. He was rushing to leave for the Bank President's monthly meeting in Hazelwood. But he greeted them warmly and invited them to sit down.

"Did I forget something, ladies?" he asked as he settled in his chair. "I thought the meeting and check presentation was Saturday."

"It is," Paula said. Paula had forgotten how intense his blue eyes were. He looked at her like he could see right through to the soul.

"Could I offer you something? I really have only a few minutes, but would you like a cup of coffee? Or I can send for some juice."

"You got chocolate?" Paula asked.

Davis was taken back but grinned when he saw Paula's mischievous look. "Chocolate. I forgot the chocolate."

"You always have chocolate to offer a lady," she told him. "Always."

"This is about that piece of chocolate cake I stole from you at Martin's party, isn't it? Chocolate. I owe you chocolate. I won't forget again. Now what can I do for you?"

"It's for me actually," Stacy said. There was a slight tremor in her voice and Paula reached over to pat her hand.

"I...I know you're in a hurry, so I'll make this quick." The quicker the better, she thought to herself.

"Do you remember some money that came up missing here at the bank over thirty years ago?"

"Of course." He now had those incredible eyes locked in a gaze with Stacy. "It's the only time we've ever been robbed! But I can't really say we were robbed because the money has been paid back with a very generous interest over the years. Why do you ask about it?"

"I took it," Stacy said and bit her bottom lip.

"I know."

Stacy stared at him, her eyes wide and disbelieving. Paula also stared and almost gagged.

"What? What do you mean, you know? Stacy, you said no one knew."

Stacy shook her head. "They couldn't. No one ever said...why did you say that, Davis?"

He sat back with a slight smile. "Dad figured it out within days. He knew it had to have been you. And he figured out why. You needed money for college. Your mother couldn't help you, and you were feeling stressed--"

"But he never said--"

Davis shook his head. "Stacy, he would have given you the money from his own account if you had asked. He really liked you, and he knew that things were looking pretty bleak for your future. He wouldn't have said a word if his life depended on it. Then when he got the first payment...well, he felt that his confidence in you was justified."

"But how could he have known it was me?"

Davis shrugged. "I don't know. He just did. One of the last things he told me was to make sure you knew everything was square if you ever mentioned it. And to assure you that he did not hold a grudge."

A sob escaped Stacy and Paula reached over to give her a hug.

"We were afraid you would have her arrested," Paula joked.

Davis squirmed uncomfortably. "Stacy, don't cry. It's over. The money's paid back. Let's just drop it. It doesn't need to go any further than this office. Dad would be pleased to know you told us. But he'd haunt me until my dying day if I did anything to make you more miserable. It's done; it's over. You've probably punished yourself more over the years than we ever could have."

"Amen to that," Paula said.

"I...I just don't know what to say," Stacy said and wiped her eyes with a tissue Paula handed her.

"Say goodbye," Davis said and stood. "I'm really late, so I've got to go. Thanks for coming in, Stacy. My dad was right about you. Listen, I'm looking forward to seeing all four of you Saturday morning."

"Yes," Paula said and steered Stacy to the door. "We'll see you then. Drive safely, Davis. Don't speed because we kept you so long."

"At least, I'd have an excuse this time," he said with a grin.

They drove to the nursing home.

"I can't believe it," Stacy said over and over. "I just cannot believe it. Wait until I tell Daniel."

They found Karen sitting in the reception area trying to spoon oatmeal into her father's mouth. Mr. Montgomery wasn't enthusiastic about eating it.

"How did it go?" she asked. Her voice was quiet, but her eyes demanded information.

"Stacy told Davis."

"And?"

"And," Stacy said, "his exact words were 'I know.' Can you believe that? I mean, can you *believe* that?"

"Yes, I can. Oh, please, Dad. Try just a little for me. Open the tunnel and let the choo-choo in."

"My princess had a unicorn."

Karen paused with the spoon in midair. "You remember that?" She looked up at Karen and Paula who were still standing. "I had this white stuffed unicorn when I was about five or six. I carried the thing everywhere. It had to have its own place at the table. I loved that thing. I can't even remember what I named it now."

Mr. Montgomery swallowed the bite of oatmeal she had managed to cram in his mouth and made a face. "Princess loved Freda."

"Freda! That's what I named it! Dad, how in the world did you remember that? Whoops!"

Mr. Montgomery yawned widely, letting the oatmeal ooze out of his mouth. Karen took the spoon and scooped it up. "Come on, Dad. Just a few more bites. Dammit, why don't they try to feed them something appetizing? This is crap. I wouldn't eat it."

"Hey," Paula said, her voice low. "Who is that man over there? He looks familiar, but I can't place him."

Karen looked and then casually spooned more oatmeal.

"Oh, that's Ryan Wardlow. I saw him here the other day."

"I knew he looked familiar," Paula said. "Why is he here?"

"His aunt's here. He's her only relative now, I guess."

"I don't remember him so he must be older." Stacy said.

Stacy and Paula took a seat across from Karen and her dad.

The man walked toward them. He smiled and nodded.

"Hello. You may not remember me but I'm Ryan Wardlow. I think I was three years ahead of you in school."

"Kenneth," Karen said. "You would have been in Kenneth's class."

"Yes," Ryan said. "I was also in Les Kimball's class. I believe his little sister Annette was a friend of yours."

"Still is," Karen informed him. "Well, I give up. Come on, Dad, you're falling asleep in your chair. Nice to see you again, Ryan."

"You, too," he said and watched her carefully.

Karen signaled to an aide. "Just let me get Dad settled, and we can leave."

"How about I take us to Wendy's for lunch," Stacy suggested.

"Sounds good. I'll only be a minute. Goodbye, Ryan."

They enjoyed a salad and then decided that since they had saved so many calories they were entitled to a Wendy's chocolate frozen dessert. They laughed like they hadn't done in days. Stacy, in particular, seemed so much at ease that she reverted to the silly side she had often displayed in school.

"Did Paula tell you?" Karen asked. "We will be riding in the car with Annette and Brent."

"Yup!" Stacy scrapped the bottom of her cup with the spoon and sucked off the last of the chocolate. "And you know what? I want a crown."

"A crown!" Paula's mouth dropped in amazement. "A crown?

Well, yeah, we need a crown. And one of those banner things. You know, it goes from the shoulder to the waist. I want one of those."

"And a bouquet!" Karen said. "I want a bouquet of flowers. It doesn't have to be as big as the queen's, but I want flowers, too."

"It should be bigger than the queen's," Stacy said. "She's the one who got us into this!"

They laughed and joked until the personnel began to give them looks.

"We better go," Paula said. "Before we get kicked out!"

"What is everyone doing this afternoon? Annette said we can't get together until around seven," Karen said. "Anybody else have any plans?"

Both Stacy and Paula shook their heads.

"I want to do some grocery shopping tomorrow and make a lunch for Raelene. She's to be back through here around noon. She doesn't want to stay though. She wants to drive as far as her youngest daughter's house tomorrow. And then drive on home on Saturday."

"I'm going to Claire's in the morning to do some laundry and eat leftover lasagna with her," Paula said. "I thought about trying to call the kids this afternoon. I haven't been able to get any of them since I've been here."

"Let's go to a movie," Karen said. "They have a new theater complex in Cullen. There's surely something worth seeing."

"Let's do it," Paula said. "I'm in the mood for a comedy."

"I want a sweet, feel good movie," Stacy said.

"I want to see someone drop dead gorgeous and hunky," Karen said with a wicked grin. "Maybe there's a Jace Collins moving showing."

Paula blushed and then turned absolutely scarlet when Stacy squealed, "Oh, he is so cute!"

Annette, Stacy, and Paula knocked on Karen's door at two minutes before seven. The smell of pizza greeted them.

"I ordered super supreme," she said. "If you don't like something, pick it off. No complaints."

"I like everything," Paula said and took a slice. "Well, not those little fishes. But I doubt they offer them here in Bonnetville anyway. Oh, yes! I love jalapenos!"

They had only begun eating when a knock on the door interrupted them. Karen flung it open, a slice of pizza drooping in her hand.

"Excuse me," the young girl in a hotel staff uniform said. "This package came today for Mrs. Paula Clifford. My supervisor said I might find her here."

"How damn, Paula! The guy sent you something else. Does he have a brother?"

"Oh." Flustered, Paula searched for her purse forgetting she had left it in her room. Then she felt in her pockets.

Karen understood. She took a couple of dollars from her own purse and gave it to the girl.

Her three friends demanded Paula open the package immediately. With trembling fingers Paula unwrapped the box and pulled out a beautiful suede and leather pantsuit in a lush dark green. The pants and jacket were of the same fabric while the turtleneck was soft cashmere in a lighter shade of green. A gold belt accented the slightly dropped waistline.

"Try it on, try it on," the three chanted.

"Okay, okay," Paula said trying to sound miffed. But she couldn't stop smiling. When she emerged from the bathroom, her smile was radiant.

"Wow," Annette said.

"It fits," Paula said.

"Like it was made for you," Karen said. "This guy is good."

"It's gorgeous," Stacy said. "And it looks so good on you."

"I think I'll wear it to the game and dance," Paula said as she twisted and turned in front of the mirror. "Do you think this would look okay to wear in the car at half-time?"

The other three hooted.

"Not fair," Annette said. "You're not supposed to look better than me. I'm the queen! No comments," she warned when she saw Karen open her mouth to speak.

"I think I will wear it. Oh, it feels so good! And I have a set of earrings and necklace the kids gave me for Christmas a couple of years ago. I'm so glad I brought them with me!"

"What about your pretty new purple suit?" Karen said. "That looks good, too."

"I'll wear it tomorrow night," Paula said. "I love them both. I'm going to take this off now before I get pizza all over it. Be right back."

The moment the bathroom door closed, Stacy and Annette leaned toward Karen.

"You said you know who her mystery guy is," Stacy said. "Tell us."

Karen pretended to zip her lips.

Annette sat back with a groan. "What a time for you to finally keep your mouth shut! Uh, uh, uh! You're still zipped closed."

"I know we're all tired," Annette said. "But we just need to briefly say what we would do with the money if we're the one chosen to get it. Paula, would you like to go first?"

"Uh, no. Let someone else go first."

"Stacy?"

Stacy gave her funny little head shake. "I honestly don't know. I think I would take Daniel to Hawaii for our next anniversary. I would let Austin go to that Space Camp he's always talking about. And I would probably buy about a dozen boxes of Girl Scout cookies. I'd put the rest in the bank for Daniel's peace of mind. He's so afraid he hasn't prepared well for us if he…well, I'd just have some money when I needed it."

"I know what I'd do," Karen said. "I've always wanted to

take a cruise around the world. That would be so cool. That's what I would do. Then maybe I'd buy all the kids something special. What about you, Annette?"

Annette smiled. "I'd take the family to spend Christmas in Switzerland or Austria. I'd rent a chateau and we'd go skiing every day for two weeks. Then I'd probably spend the rest on Brent's campaign. Come on, Paula. You must have thought about this."

Paula shook her head. "Not really. Well, I guess the first thing I would do is buy groceries. Lots of groceries! I've always said my idea of being rich was being able to go into the grocery store and get everything on my list. Then I'd give some to the Make a Wish Foundation. I love what they do. I'd use some to self-publish a novel I wrote. No one wants to publish it, but I like it. I don't know what I'd do with the rest. Hang on to it, I guess."

Annette nodded. "See that wasn't so hard. Well, I suggest we meet around one tomorrow and sum up this thing. That will give us plenty of time to get ready for the open house tomorrow night."

"What time does it start?" Karen started clearing away the pizza box and crumbs.

"Five. There's to be free hamburgers and hot dogs. Then a chance for visiting before the dance starts at eight. I was hoping Brent and the kids could be here for that, but Brent is scheduled for an appearance at the University of Texas tomorrow night. So I'm free if you three want to be my dates."

"We'll be there," Paula said. She picked up her box with the

252

pantsuit and headed for the door. "I want to try and call the kids again. It's like they are all avoiding me."

Stacy stood also. "I want to call Daniel, too. Goodnight."

"Hey, Paula," Karen called. "Can I borrow that pantsuit? I can break it in for you tomorrow night. Paula! I'll take that as a no," Karen said to Annette when they didn't hear a reply.

"I'd say you take that correctly," Annette said with a laugh as she got ready to go, too.

Paula was frustrated. She tried calling Becca's apartment but all she got was the answering machine. Then she called the lab where Becca and her husband both worked. She was told that Becca and Jim were taking a quick trip and wouldn't be back until the following Wednesday. It was so unlike Becca not to keep her informed.

She had no better luck reaching Troy. Again, all she got was his answering machine. She finally broke down and called the airline where she was told Mr. Clifton would not be available for the next four days.

That left Ricky. He answered on the first ring.

"Thank goodness I have one child I can find," she said.

"Hi, Mom. Actually, you just caught me. I have an evening class."

"Oh. Well, I won't keep you. I was just wondering how you are and what your plans are for the weekend."

"I'm fine. Uh, the weekend. Well, I hope to spend it with

some of my favorite people. That's the plan anyway."

"Oh, okay. Where would that be?"

"What? Yeah, I'm coming. Sorry, Mom. I've got to get to that class. Talk to you soon."

It wasn't until she hung up that Paula realized that nine-thirty in the evening was much too late for a class to be beginning.

Chapter 26

Decisions and Indecisions

Paula loaded her laundry in the car, thanked Claire, and drove away. She didn't return to the hotel however. Instead, she drove around the country looking at places she hadn't seen since she was a child. As she drove, she thought about the past week. She had learned so much about her friends and revealed even more about herself. She wasn't certain she was any happier knowing or doing any of it. But it had been an enlightening experience. And it had been wonderful being with Stacy, Karen, and Annette. It was amazing how closely bonded they were even after thirty years. It was also incredible, she realized, that it was the first time in all those years they had been together at the same time. She had seen Karen a couple of times and Annette once. But she had only spoken on the phone to Stacy and wrote letters to them all.

Who would get the money? Paula had no idea who it would be. She knew who she wanted to vote for, but she didn't know if she had the courage to do what she had in mind. Who was really deserving? They had all done good. But they had also all done things that were bad. Why didn't they just split the money four ways? Surely, that would be fair. It would be over ten thousand dollars each, still enough for them to do something.

For some reason she didn't understand, Paula wanted to cry. Her eyes watered and her nose burned as she fought to keep the tears from winning. She decided to return to the hotel and try once again to call her children though she doubted she would reach either of them. She would also try one more time to call Jace. She had tried twice yesterday but got only his voice mail. Surely, he was back in range now. Was his not getting in touch with her significant? Did it mean that maybe he finally realized their relationship should...what relationship? They were friends, good friends. But that's all it had been. That silly Karen had got her thinking that maybe it was okay to...but she wouldn't think about that now. Even as she resolved to push those thoughts aside, she wondered what it meant when he got her the motel room and sent the flowers and fruit basket. And what about the beautiful pantsuit?

Oh, it was too confusing! She hadn't felt so awful since she was in high school and had her first crush on Davis Griffin. She wasn't a teenager any more, for crying out loud. She was a middle-aged woman with grown children. She was...still young at heart and vulnerable to the attentions of a very desirable young man.

Maybe a good cry would cleanse the soul and the mind. Then

maybe she could think about what to do next.

Annette punched in a different station on the radio and turned onto the main highway. Another silly luncheon with a bunch of snooty, giddy women! Maybe she wasn't cut out for the campaign trail after all. It was one thing to get involved for a candidate you could get away from at the end of the day. But she wondered if she had the stamina and desire to stick with it for months, perhaps even years. Still, she wanted Brent to be elected governor. She believed in her husband. She knew he could do the job and do it well. She would see to it.

It was his darn secretary that bothered her so much. Maybe it was time for her to have her own secretary. She had been thinking about that a lot the past week. If she got the money, she could afford to hire someone she liked and trusted.

Who would get the money? She had thought of all the conversations she, Karen, Paula, and Stacy had had over the last week. Why had she thought that after all these years, it would be a cut and dried decision? It was far from that. In some ways, they were equally deserving. Even their sins had some equity. Except for hers. No one had been able to top hers. Her only consolation was that she could blame her mother.

Maybe she was cut out to be a politician after all. Weren't they supposed to put the blame on others?

Annette switched channels again and sped up a bit. She wanted to get back to the hotel and make a list of everyone's deeds, good and bad. She had a feeling if she did that, it would be obvious to her who should get the money.

But first, she wanted to call Brent to make sure he and the kids would be in Bonnetville early the next day. And she wanted him to agree that she needed her own secretary. Because if his tyrant of a secretary gave her one more speaking assignment...the next murder she committed might be premeditated.

Stacy hugged Raelene bye and waved until the car was out of sight. Her eyes burned and her face was swollen after she and her sister pampered themselves with a good long cry. She wanted Raelene to spend the night, but her sister wanted to get back on the road. Stacy wondered if she would ever see her brother-in-law again, and the knowledge that his death would be soon made her start crying again.

She wanted to get in the car and drive home to Daniel and Austin. She wanted to snuggle next to Daniel and forget about all the worries and problems that existed in the world. She didn't want to be bothered with deciding who should have the money and why. She wished she hadn't heard about all the things her friends had done. That wasn't exactly true. She was proud of the good things. But the bad things...it only made hers seem that much worse.

Who would get her vote? There was only one choice so far as she was concerned. She had known that before they had even gotten together. There was only one person's whose good deeds had offset the bad. That was her opinion, of course. But her vote was as good as cast.

Karen crushed out the cigarette as soon as she took the first puff. She sat in her car down the road from the house she had lived in the first eighteen years of her life. She didn't know who owned it now, but they had kids. All sorts of play equipment littered the yard.

Life had been so easy then. She hadn't realized it at the time, of course. Kid never did. But in those days, you did what your parents told you to do, ignored what your brothers told you to do, and did whatever else you could get away with. You enjoyed the freedom of life rather than being burdened by it.

Thirty years ago, Karen never would have suspected she would have been married three times and have seven kids. Small town and country girls didn't do that. They married their high school sweetheart, had three or four kids, and celebrated their fiftieth anniversaries with a trip to Hawaii.

She didn't want to go to Hawaii. She wanted to take a cruise around the world. She had wanted to do that for years. The money would give her that freedom.

The trouble was she didn't deserve it any more than the other three. But who should get the money? Screw the confessions. Everyone did wrong. It was how you handled the mistakes that mattered, and they had all handled them as well as could be expected. Who had done the best though? That's what she needed to focus on.

Well, hell, that shot her out of the saddle.

She started the engine and pulled back onto the road. You couldn't live in the past. But Bonnetville wasn't such a bad place to live. She had thought so years ago. Like the others, she hadn't wanted to be stuck here. Now it seemed safe and comfortable.

She was too young to be so sentimental. And too old to be so philosophical.

She knew who she should vote for but she couldn't think of why she shouldn't vote for the others. She needed a sign, something to tip the scales in one direction.

What she really needed was a drink and some male company.

She sighed. She would settle for a Pepsi and a phone call.

They met in Annette's room at three. She greeted them at the door but bustled around the room and talked non-stop instead of sitting down with them.

"All right. I made a list of each of our accomplishments and each of our...uh, I called them setbacks. After all, they aren't really failures, are they? We've all made the best of it and gone on. They've been learning experiences. And I mention what we would do with the money. So! Here's a copy for each of you. I'll give you a few minutes to look over it."

Karen, Paula, and Stacy exchanged looks and then glanced dubiously at the list Annette thrust in their hands. What happened to their cool, brisk, efficient Mrs. Future First Lady? She was being efficient, they would give her that. But she was anything but cool. She was downright maniacal.

They looked at the list and scanned it quickly.

Paula

Accomplishments:	*Wrote and published two children's books*
	Received an award for one book
	Served as a state representative on the
	National Read Now committee
	Organized relief centers after a tornado
	and grass fire
	Talked a would be sniper out of hurting
	anyone
	Adopted a daughter from China
Setbacks:	*Tried to poison husband*
	Framed a woman for shoplifting
Spend Money:	*Groceries*
	Donate to Make A Wish Foundation
	Self-Publish a Novel
	Save remaining amount

Stacy

Accomplishments:	*Donated kidney to nephew*
	Organized tutoring program at school
	Served on school Accountability Committee
	Taught Sunday school

Paid back stolen money with interest

Setbacks: *Stole $2000 from Bonnetville Bank*

Spend Money: *Go to Hawaii*

Send son to Space Camp

Save remaining amount

Karen

Accomplishments: *Public singing*

Saved senior housing center

Kept hospital open

Served as PTA president

Served as Scout leader

Rescued woman from burning house

Setbacks: *Embezzled money from clients*

Had an affair while married

Kept children from grandparents

Spent Money: *Take cruise around world*

Buy something for children

Annette

Accomplishments: *Graduated college with honors*

Served as mayor

Organized and directed relief operations

    after tornado

Established two dozen public libraries

Served on various boards and committees for

education reform and health care

Setbacks: *Destroyed life of a child*

Destroyed senator's career

Spent Money: *Christmas vacation with family in Europe*

Help finance husband's campaign

"You have got to be kidding!" Karen waved the paper in the air. "This is a bunch of bullarky!"

Annette's eyes widened. "What are you talking about? This is exactly what we've said all week."

"You've reduced thirty years into a few stark, bleak lines! Everything we've done that is good reads like a grocery list. The failures...failures, Annie. Call them what they are, they're just words on a line. And how we would spend the money...I won't even touch that. How are we supposed to decide who really deserves the money? Count up who has the most accomplishments and the fewest failures? Excuse me. Setbacks." She crumpled the paper with quick, angry jabs and tossed it toward the trash can. "How dare you be so pompous!"

Annette sank on the bed, breathing heavily. "I just was trying to summarize everything. Make it convenient for us to vote. I...I wasn't trying to--"

"And what was it you said? Destroyed a child's life? Hell, Annette, it's called an abortion. At least, call it what it is."

"I don't like to use that word!" Annette's face twisted in anguish.

"Stop it." Paula's voice was quiet but firm. "Just stop it. Okay, I admit the list seems impersonal and...well, unnecessary. Like Karen said, it's just a list. We need to remember the emotions we felt as we discussed these things. We need to think about how we were affected at the time. Our vote should be based on gut feelings not a list."

"I just thought it would help." Annette snatched a tissue from the box on the table and blew her nose.

"It was a considerate gesture," Stacy said. "It's just a reminder, isn't it, Annette? We don't need to get upset over something like this, right? Come on, let's forget it. We don't want to end our week with hard feelings. It's not worth it. No amount of money is worth that."

"Oh." Paula smoothed her blouse and brushed away lint no one else could see. "That reminds me of something I wanted to suggest. Now just hear me out, okay. I...I was thinking today. We've all done some great things. And we've all done some not so great things. Maybe we should just divide the money equally and we would each--"

"Not a chance!" Karen stood over Paula and glared at her.

"Okay!" Paula held up her hands and shrugged. " Forget it."

"Damn straight."

"Okay, Karen. Jeez."

"Actually," Annette said, "more than one person could get the money. Realistically, all four of us could get a vote. Or two of us could get two votes."

It was good to see Annette calm and in control again. They gladly turned their attention to her."

"Well," said Karen. "If two people get two votes, then those two can share equally. If everyone gets a vote, we vote again. If it's still a four-way tie, I guess we would share it four ways. If one person gets one vote and another gets three votes, the one with three votes gets the money. Agreed?"

"Agreed," Paula said.

"Agreed," Stacy said.

Annette shrugged.

"Okay. No more talk of just splitting the money. We voted on it."

"Fine." Annette bounced off the bed and reached for four little squares of paper. She handed one to each woman. "Write your choice on this paper and fold it over."

"Wait," Paula said. She squirmed in her seat. "I...I'd like to think about this a little more."

"What?" Karen stared in disbelief.

"Actually, I want a little more time, too," Stacy said, her voice calm and firm. "What's the hurry? We can take them with us tomorrow and let Davis tally the results."

"Sounds good to me," Paula said.

Karen muttered curses under her breath and slipped the paper in her pocket.

"Then I guess we're done here," she said. "I'm going to get ready for tonight. Jeez, Louise. You three are all crackers!"

Chapter 27

Fearless Foursome's Final Fling

Everyone's good humor was restored by the time they were ready to leave for the school. The open house that started Homecoming Weekend was held in the high school gym. Paula, clad in her new lilac pant suit, offered to drive them all. She hadn't felt so pretty and excited in…she couldn't remember when. She, Karen, and Annette piled into her Chevy and drove over to pick up Stacy.

"I'm glad we're all going together," Stacy said when she joined them in the car. "I think I would be so nervous walking in by myself."

"I would be, too, if I were you," Karen said. "Everyone will be thrilled to see you, the little darling of our class. Now most of them will run from me."

Stacy blushed. It was true she had been class favorite all through school. But a lot had changed in those years since. The past week had proved that.

"I hope there is better food tonight that we used to offer in the concession stands," Stacy said as she hooked her seat belt.

Karen frowned. "What are you talking about?"

"Don't you remember?" Stacy asked. "We sold some of the weirdest things. We were so embarrassed when we had to work in the concession stands during home games."

"Oh, poor you!" Paula laughed as she signaled and pulled away from the curb. "You three only had fifteen minute assignments because you were a cheerleader or in the band. I had to do a whole hour. Sometimes more if not many kids showed up like they were supposed to."

"But what did we sell that was so bad?" Annette asked. "Burgers and hot dogs?"

"Hot dogs, yes," Paula said. "Never burgers though. They were too expensive back then. Different classes or clubs were assigned to bring in sandwiches. The shop class always brought in potted meat and mayonnaise on white bread."

All four of them burst out laughing.

"That is pretty bad," Annette agreed.

"No, what was bad," Paula said "is that they always sold!"

They laughed again and Stacy bounced up and down waving a hand. "And I remember the corn chips with chili on them."

"Hey, that's good stuff," Karen protested. "Put cheese and onions on top and that's a meal. I make that every so often during the winter. My girls love it."

"Remember those huge whole dill pickles?" Paula asked. "Fifty cents each. We sold two gallon jars every game. All the kids walked around munching those pickles."

"Oh! Oh! Oh!" Annette said. "The lemons! Remember the lemons?"

"Lemons?" Karen asked with a frown.

"Yes!" Stacy exclaimed. "With the peppermint stick in the middle!"

"Right," Paula added as she pulled into the school parking lot. "We cut lemons in half, put a long peppermint stick in the middle, and everyone walked around sucking the lemon juice through the peppermint stick. Twenty-five cents and one of our best sellers!"

They walked in together still laughing. At first no one noticed them. Then a man who was standing at a microphone on a makeshift stage at the far end of the gym faked a wild display of surprise.

"Ladies and gentlemen! Ex-Bonnetville Warriors! Can I believe my eyes? Look who just graced our little gathering. I do believe it is…the Fearless Foursome!"

"Shit," Karen said as all eyes turned toward them.

"Oh, my gosh," Paula gasped.

"Is that Arnie Doppelganger?" Stacy asked. "Why is he using a microphone? He never needed one before."

"Good photo-op," Paula whispered to Annette.

Annette smiled, squared her shoulders, and waved around the room. "Be nice," she said out of the corner of her mouth

"Do you remember that funky dance these girls did at the Senior Class Talent Show, folks? Let's encourage them to perform again. Come on, let's hear it!"

Stacy gasped and Paula paled. They both shook their heads and waved off the chorus of "Dance! Dance! Dance!"

Karen and Annette smiled and tried to follow Stacy and Paula out of the limelight.

"Come on, somebody put on that song. "It was 'My Guy', wasn't it? Come on, girls. You're among family here!"

"Then you're all grounded," Karen snarled through clenched teeth

"Dance! Dance! Dance!" the crowd chanted and cleared a space in the middle of the floor.

"What's wrong? Have the Fearless Foursome suddenly become the Fearsome Foursome? That's all right, girls! We all lose our stuff when we get older."

The music started, a blare that almost took their breaths away. Paula glared toward Arnie on the stage.

"I just remembered," she told the other three. "He lost out to us. His Elvis impression bombed, and he was eliminated in the round against us."

"Oh, a vendetta," Annette said wisely.

"Yeah, well," Paula said. She straightened the top of her new suit, shook her hands loosely at her side, and nodded toward the middle of the floor."

"Let's go, girls."

"You're kidding!" Stacy was ready to go all right. She was ready to either go back to her niece's house or pass out right where she stood.

"You're right," Karen said, her grin definitely impish. "I say we show this clodhopping clown a thing or two."

"That's what I'm worried about!" Stacy wailed. "I'm too old to make a total complete fool of myself."

"My dear," Karen said stroking an imaginary mustache, "You're never too old for that."

Annette, Karen, and Paula grabbed Stacy and hustled to the middle of the floor amid catcalls and applause. Then, as though the years had faded back to high school, the four middle-aged women fell right into the dance they had done so long ago. They twisted, gyrated, swooped, turned, wiggled, and shook in an almost perfect synchronization. Once the music was over, the crowd applauded and laughed and called congratulations. The Fearless Foursome gave exaggerated bows and finally managed to blend into the crowd.

"That was fun!" Karen said. She breathed hard. "I need to take up aerobic dancing. That's good exercise."

"Irene!" Paula walked over to Irene who was sitting in a chair against the wall. She looked better tonight than Paula had seen her. There was more color in her face, and her eyes sparkled with excitement. She was wearing a cute blouse with a matching scarf around her head.

"How are you?" Paula asked and took the seat next to Irene.

"I'm feeling pretty well tonight. And I got a very optimistic call from my doctor today. They're think I may need only a couple more chemo sessions and expect me to be in full remission."

"That's wonderful!" Stacy had taken the seat on the other side of Irene. "Have you eaten? Could I get you a burger or something?"

"Oh, no. Mark is around somewhere. I'll eat when he's ready. Y'all sure looked good out there! My gosh, none of you have lost it! Serves old Arnie right. He was trying to embarrass you, and you made him look like an idiot."

"That was never hard to do if I remember correctly," Karen said. "Now they're doing a line dance! I thought that had gone out a long time ago."

"Old traditions die hard here in Bonnetville," Irene said with a laugh. "And besides they really are fun."

"Then let's go dance it," Annette said and offered her hand to Irene.

"What?"

"Sure. Come on. Are you up to it?" Annette wiggled her fingers to encourage Irene.

Irene hesitated. Then with a laugh, she grabbed Annette's hand and allowed herself to be led to the floor. The five women fell into the back line and followed the movements of the people in front of them. By the end of the dance, they were laughing and fanning their hot faces. Mark Crawford seemed to materialize out of nowhere and took his wife's arm.

"Baby, you sure you should be doing that?"

"Why not! It was fun. Will you listen to that? Who is

running the music? A waltz?"

"I bet you two can do a pretty mean waltz," Paula said.

Irene looked up at Mark with a hopeful expression. "I know you don't particularly like to dance, honey, but--"

"I can dance with the best of them," he said and danced her away.

"Irene looks radiant tonight," Stacy said. "I'm glad she's having a good time."

"I hope we all have a good time. Right now, I'd like a good burger. Think we can find one?" Karen asked.

"Probably not," Paula said. "But we can probably find a burger. Can't guarantee how good it will be?"

"Suppose I can get a lemon and peppermint stick with it?"

Laughing, Paula shoved Karen toward the food line.

It was fun to see old friends and try to guess who others were. They enjoyed meeting spouses and children of former classmates. They visited with a couple of ancient teachers who were attending. But after a couple of hours, Paula and Stacy had been entertained enough.

"I wonder if Karen and Annette would mind," Paula said when they both expressed a desire to leave.

"Annette's brother is here. I'm sure he could give them a ride back to the motel."

"I'll go see if they want to leave or stay."

Paula was back in a minute. "They both say they will hang around a little longer. Let's go."

When Paula pulled up in front of Nina's house, Stacy gasped.

"What is it?"

"I'm sure I just saw Daniel walk in front of the living room window!"

"There's an extra car," Paula pointed out. "Is it his?"

"No. It's Perry's. Perry's going to see his dad tomorrow. Oh, I know! Daniel and Austin rode here with Perry so we wouldn't have two cars. Yippee! Come on in and meet my guys."

Paula could see immediately why Stacy was so in love with Daniel. He greeted her like she was the most cherished person on earth. They embraced and exchanged fond kisses. Austin broke away from a board game with Nina's daughter to greet his mother.

"Mom, you look super," he said. "I missed you this week. Dad's not as good a cook as you are."

Paula left quickly as she could without appearing rude. She knew that Stacy didn't mind. Stacy had eyes only for her husband and son.

Her cell phone rang just as she stepped out of the elevator on the fifth floor. She felt weak in the knees when she heard his voice.

"I'm at the airport right now," Jace said. "But I wanted to say hello and tell you how much I've missed hearing your voice every day. I've got almost an hour before we board. Fill me in on what's happening there."

They talked until Jace had to leave. It wasn't until they hung up that Paula wondered which airport he had been calling from.

Chapter 28

Friends to the End

Stacy was waiting in the parking lot when Annette drove up with Karen and Paula.

"Well," Stacy said smiling brightly. "This is it. The big day."

"Has everyone cast their vote?" Karen asked, skipping any preliminaries.

No one answered and she glared around at them. "Well?"

Stacy nodded. Annette held one of the square papers neatly folded in half.

"I've got mine," Paula said.

"Okay, then. I guess it's time."

"Just a minute."

Stacy held back and the others turned to her.

"I was thinking."

"No, we are not splitting the money four ways. We've already been over that, Stacy."

Stacy shook her head impatiently. "That not what I was going to say. Just hush, Karen. I was thinking. We've enjoyed getting together, haven't we? I've loved seeing you all again."

"It has been great," Annette told her with a smile. "I'm going to miss you all more this time than I did when we left high school. I better understand now what I will be missing."

"Me, too," Paula said.

"So you want to plan another reunion in thirty years?" Karen asked. "Maybe have another pact?"

"No, I want to suggest a get together say at least every other year. I know we're all busy and time gets away so fast. But I think it would be a great idea if we got together even for a long weekend. Maybe we could take turns going to each other's houses. What do you think?"

"I think it's a great idea," Paula said. "And I think we should promise right now to stay in better touch with each other. We should call each other at least every few weeks. And it's not going to hurt any of you to write a letter. Kar-en," she added pointedly.

Karen grinned. "And everyone should send me a present on my birthday."

"Seriously, can we do that?" Stacy asked.

"I don't see why not," Annette said. "It's a wonderful idea, Stacy. I agree with you. And Paula. We do need to stay in touch better."

"What if you're Mrs. Governor?" Karen asked. "Might you be too busy for slumber parties and shopping sprees?"

"I will not. I hope I am Mrs. Governor as you say. Oh, and by the way. I hope all of you will be at the press conference this afternoon. It's at three at the high school. We thought that would be a good time before we got together for an early dinner at the hotel. I'm really excited for you to meet my family."

"Me, too," Stacy said.

Karen dug a pocket calendar out of her purse. "Okay, this is for the next three years. What day do we want to shoot for?"

"Let's leave it open," Paula smiled. "There's no way we can know now when we'll be free. Let's just make a pact that we will get together."

She held out a hand, palm down. Stacy put a hand on top of Paula's. Annette added a hand, and finally Karen put her hand on top. They moved their hands gently up and down.

"What do we say?" Paula asked.

"Friends forever!" Karen said.

"Friends forever!" they chanted together and threw their hands up in the air.

Linking arms, they made an impressive sight walking in the bank and up the stairs.

The Vote

Davis welcomed the ladies back to his office. He had been looking forward to this morning and was excited that they would all be together again. He had taken the precaution of having double fudge nut brownies specially ordered from Town Market and an assortment of juices and coffee available. Their reaction delighted him.

"Davis! You sweet man!" Karen squealed. She snatched up a napkin and chose a brownie. "You must make some woman a wonderful husband."

"Well," he shrugged. "To be honest, Peggy isn't much into chocolate. But she's northerner, so what does she know? If you tell me chocolate is a woman's staple, I would never dream of depriving you. Here, Annie, have a brownie. Paula, Stacy, help yourselves. Hell, I'll send out for more if I need to."

"How did we let this man get away?" Karen said with a laugh.

"I don't remember him being this gracious in high school," Paula said with a wicked grin. "In fact, I distinctively remember him once telling me that a certain piece of Larry Phillip's birthday cake would make me grossly fat and give me pimples."

Davis shook his head and stared at this coffee mug, clearly seeing something the past.

"Gee, I really wanted that piece of cake," he said.

The ladies hooted with laugher, and Stacy got up to put another brownie before Davis.

Once the food was gone and the laughter had died down, Davis looked at them seriously.

"Are we ready, ladies? I've got the check right here. I just need a name to go on it."

"Ah," Annette said, dramatically putting a finger to the side of her nose in a look of studious reflection. "And the big winner is…drum roll, please."

He looked at each of the four in turn. "Yes?"

Stacy walked over to the coffee table and picked up an empty mug. She stuck a piece of folded paper in it and handed the mug to Paula who did the same thing. Annette and Karen likewise added slips of folded papers. Then Karen put the mug before Davis.

"This is your moment of glory, Dave old boy," she said sitting back down. "We've each one recorded our choice for winner. You get to read the names and tally the votes. In case of a tie we'll need two checks."

Davis grinned and held the mug between his hands. "Well, this is an honor! I mean that. I just wish my dad could be here today. He always wondered which of you girls would end up with what he called the fortune. I accept this honor on his behalf."

"Yeah, yeah, yeah," Karen said, airily waving a hand. "Get on with it. This is a busy day. The parade, the reception, the dinner, the game, the dance. We can't sit here all day. There's hair to do, nails to polish. Get on with it, my good man."

Davis, grinning, inclined his head with mock dignity. "As you wish, Oh Most Patient One. Here we go. The first one out of the cup is...Paula!"

They gave a brief, solemn applause. Paula smiled, but it was strained. Davis imagined they were all nervous. He was glad he hadn't had to vote. It would have been a very difficult decision.

He took out another paper and unfolded it. "And the second one is...Paula!" He smiled at her, but she was studying her knee where she was picked at some invisible lint or thread. The other three women gave a collective 'ooh'.

"Well, you're in, Paula," Annette pointed out. "Now is it for the whole thing or half? Go on, Davis pull another."

This time he read simply, "Paula."

They applauded again.

"It's yours, Paula!" Stacy said, smiling and reaching over to hug her friend. "You truly do deserve it."

"There's one paper left," Karen pointed out.

"Do we have to read it," Paula asked suddenly. She looked around at each of her friends. "I don't want anyone to feel bad."

"Nope, got to read it," Karen insisted. "It's only fair. I personally want to see if anyone regarded my triumphs."

"But--"

Paula wanted to protest further but she caught Davis's eye. He held up the remaining slip of paper and they exchanged glances. She read the rebuff in his eyes.

"Well, ladies, what do I do? Read it or let it go?"

"Read it, dammit," Karen insisted.

He shook his head slightly, dropped the last paper back in the mug, and said, "Paula."

Annette, Karen, and Stacy all looked at Paula, each with a different expression. Paula's face flamed.

"You voted for yourself? Is that legal? Hell, I could have done that?" Karen wadded up her napkin and aimed at the trash missing it by two feet.

Annette smiled. "Of course, it's legal, Karen. You were free to vote for whoever you wanted. Obviously, you wanted Paula. It doesn't matter anyway. Paula would have won with or without her own vote. So congratulations, Paula! I honestly, truly think you deserve it."

"I--" Paula tried to speak.

"Well, I think she deserved it, too," Karen fumed. "Obviously, that's why I voted for her. But to vote for yourself--"

"Well," Davis said, smoothly interrupting the potential argument. "How do I make out this check, Paula? Shall I put Paula Clifton or Paula Lowe Clifton? Or have you gone back to Paula Lowe?" He paused with his pen in hand, waiting for her answer.

She smiled again, this time for real. "Make it out to Irene Crawford."

Beside her, Stacy gasped. "That is exactly what I might have expected you to do," Stacy said. Tears threatened to choke off her words. She breathed deeply. "If I had thought about it, that is exactly what I would have guessed from you."

"I don't know why," Paula said dryly. "I was always the selfish one."

She clenched her lips together and gave a slight shake of her head as though to clear it from something.

"Please. I've been thinking a lot this week. The most important thing in life is family. Family. And that includes great friends as well as those you are born to or have given birth to. You are all a very important part of my family. The next most important thing is health. I have that. Irene doesn't at the moment.

The next most important thing as I see it is a sense of decency. According to my own standards, I am one of the richest women in the world. I may not have much money and never have had, but you can't get much better than what I do have. You've all earned that money just as much as I have. Probably more. You've all proved that this week. I tried to talk you into splitting it in four ways because I already knew what I wanted to do. But I couldn't speak for all of you. I still say we can divide it, but I'm giving whatever I get to Irene."

"Well, I don't want any of it," Karen said fiercely.

Annette shook her head, smiling. Stacy dabbed away tears.

"Then please, Davis, make that check out to Irene Crawford."

"All of it?"

"All of it."

"Every bit of it?"

"Every penny."

"You know, Paula, there would be nothing wrong with you keeping some. Even five thousand would be a comfortable nest egg, and it would still give Irene a very generous gift."

Paula shook her head. By now, the tears flooded her eyes and she blinked hard to keep them there.

"You don't understand. I don't want the money. I never wanted it. All I ever wanted in life was to be happy. And I am. I say we either divide it four ways or we give the whole bit to Irene."

Annette held up a hand. "I vote for Irene."

"Second," Stacy said.

They all looked at Karen who was still staring at Paula. "You've always got to show up the rest of us, don't you? Hell, yes, give it to Irene! Serves us all right for being such money grabbing bitches all these years."

"Speak for yourself," Paula retorted but she was smiling.

Davis shook his head and wrote "Irene Crawford" on the check.

"She's going to want to know where this came from," he said. "She's written a thank you note for every donation she knows about. One this size...I have to tell her something. She's not going to be happy with an anonymous gift."

Paula looked around at the other three. "Tell her it's from the Fearless Foursome."

They left the bank arm in arm, just as they had done over thirty years earlier. They were a bit more subdued, but age and maturity tend to do that to people.

"Well, well, well," Karen said significantly as she stared at a car parked in the lot. A very handsome man leaned against it watching and smiling.

Paula gasped and froze.

"Isn't that...it is! That's Jace Collins!" Stacy squealed.

"Who?" Annette stared. "Jace Collins, the actor? What in the world would he be doing in Bonnetville?"

"Oh I think he might be here to claim a certain love of his

life," Karen said. Her impish grin was directed at Paula.

"I can't believe he's--" Paula placed a hand over her heart and took a deep breath. Standing by another car parked beside him were a lovely young lady and three young men.

"Hey, Mom!" one yelled. "I told you I was spending the weekend with some of my favorite people."

"Jace," Paula whispered. "Becca, Jim, Troy, Ricky!" A sob escaped. "I told you I am the richest woman in the world!"

Jace Collins straightened and waited to see if he was as welcome as he hoped to be. He took a few tentative steps toward them.

"Get 'em, tiger!" Karen said, shoving Paula forward.

"What?" Stacy said, confused. "You mean...that's your secret. I mean, he's...oh, wow, Paula!"

But Paula was running toward the actor. He ran to meet her and caught her up in a swing and embrace. They were still kissing when Annette, Stacy, and Karen reached them.

Paula made the introductions. Jace politely shook each of their hands while keeping one arm around Paula. It was both a protective and possessive gesture. Paula's children gathered for the greetings.

"It is a pleasure to meet you," Jace told them. His smile was even more dynamic in person than on the big screen. "I hope to see each of you this evening. I assume," he said glancing down at Paula, "that I'm invited to all your homecoming festivities."

"Absolutely," Karen said before Paula had a chance to answer.

"That's cool. Really cool," she added, not caring that she sounded like her twins.

He smiled and nodded. "Well, then I think the six of us," he said as his look included Paula's children, "will have a picnic and Paula can show me around her old stomping grounds. If that's all right with you, darling." He smiled at Paula who could only nod her agreement. "I'll look forward to meeting you and your families at dinner," he said to the three other women.

Annette nodded. "That would be great. In fact, I see Brent and the kids pulling up at the park."

"We'll see you in a few hours then," Paula said, at last finding her voice.

Jace helped her in the car and closed the door. He turned back to Paula's three friends who stared, not caring they were acting like star-struck teenagers.

"Oh, this is too perfect," Stacy said. "I may cry."

"Not again," Karen groaned. "You know, Jace, I guessed about you and Paula. I read a thing in a magazine that said you were hot-to-trot for some older woman who wrote children's books. I mean, come on. Who else could it be?"

He favored her with one of his smiles. "Good deduction. I was hoping she would tell you about me, but I am still having trouble convincing her that I am sincere in my affections."

"Oh, I think you've got her," Karen said. "She's all yours for the asking."

"Good!" Jace Collins patted his jacket pocket. "Good thing I brought the ring. Later, ladies."

They drove off leaving the three friends to stare after them.

Stacy did a little dance. "He brought a ring! How romantic is that?"

Annette waved across the street and turned to give Stacy and Karen quick hugs.

"I'll see you two later. Right now, I want to hug my own romantic guy."

Karen and Stacy watched her dash across the street and embrace her husband.

"Well," Karen said. "I guess that just leaves you and me. What are we going to do until the parade?"

"Actually," Stacy said apologetically. "Daniel and Austin got in last night. I need to get back to the house."

Karen nodded. "Sure you do. I'm looking forward to meeting them."

Stacy's brow wrinkled with concern. "Why don't you come with me? You can meet them now, and we can have lunch somewhere."

Karen shook her head. "No, baby, go on. I'm fine. I've got a call to make. You go on."

"Are you sure? Can't I give you a ride? It's too far to walk to the hotel."

"Nope." Karen tugged a cell phone from her purse. "Scat. I have a very important call to make. I'm sure there will be a ride attached to it."

"You're sure?"

"Will you get out of here? This is personal and private. Scram!"

Laughing, Stacy embraced Karen and started to leave. She came back and kissed Karen's cheek.

"Would you have taken the money?" Stacy asked.

"Sure."

Stacy studied her and then smiled. "I don't believe you."

"Why not? Wouldn't you have taken it?"

Stacy nodded. "I would."

"You would!"

"Yes. Then I would have divided it into four and put a check in a birthday card to each of you. You can't refuse a gift. But...Paula's way is better. Irene needs it more than any of us do."

Karen nodded. "Good thing we didn't start another pact," she said. "Paula would already have the jump on us."

"She wouldn't have counted it," Stacy said. "Karen, we can't, absolutely cannot, let another thirty years go by without seeing each other. Promise me we'll get together."

"We all agreed. I guarantee we'll have another get together. And soon. Goodbye. I'm punching in my number now. Bye!"

Karen almost didn't speak when he answered. But she took a deep breath and plunged in. "Hey, I'd be happy to let you take me to lunch. Work till noon? That's not so bad. Sure I can help. I know loads about contracting. Well, I can spell it anyway. Great.

But I'm on foot. You will? I'll be waiting outside the bank."

She closed the cell phone and dropped it back in her purse.

Paula had spoken volumes of wisdom in Davis's office. But she hadn't said anything Karen didn't already know. Stacy and Annette either. But they had all realized for the first time that they truly were a family. And they had wealth that far exceeded money.

Each of them had walked out of that bank richer than when they had entered. They were now making a new investment in life. They had come of age.

Karen took a crumpled pack of cigarettes from her purse and held them toward the sun.

"Here's to good friends!" she said.

Then she dropped the pack into the trash can and walked to the curb as a red pick-up truck pulled up.

"Did you know?" she said as she climbed in and reached for the seat belt. "Today is the first day of the rest of our lives."

"Long live us all!" Ryan said beside her.

ABOUT THE AUTHOR

Though Texan by birth, Sheila Loyd Campbell has lived in the mountains of central Colorado for many years. She has been writing almost from the time she first learned to form letters but only started publishing in 2012. Since then she has been working to make up for lost time. *Friends*Enemies* is her fourteenth book.

Her husband Jim is a rancher, and they enjoy spending time with their children Katy, Jason, and Jill. Other than writing, Sheila's other interests include her animals, reading, some crafts, and taking online courses. She is an avid fan of the Colorado Rockies professional baseball team. She is also an active member of The Church of Jesus Christ of Latter-day Saints.

Printed in Great Britain
by Amazon